Coloring Book For Adults To Relieve Stress

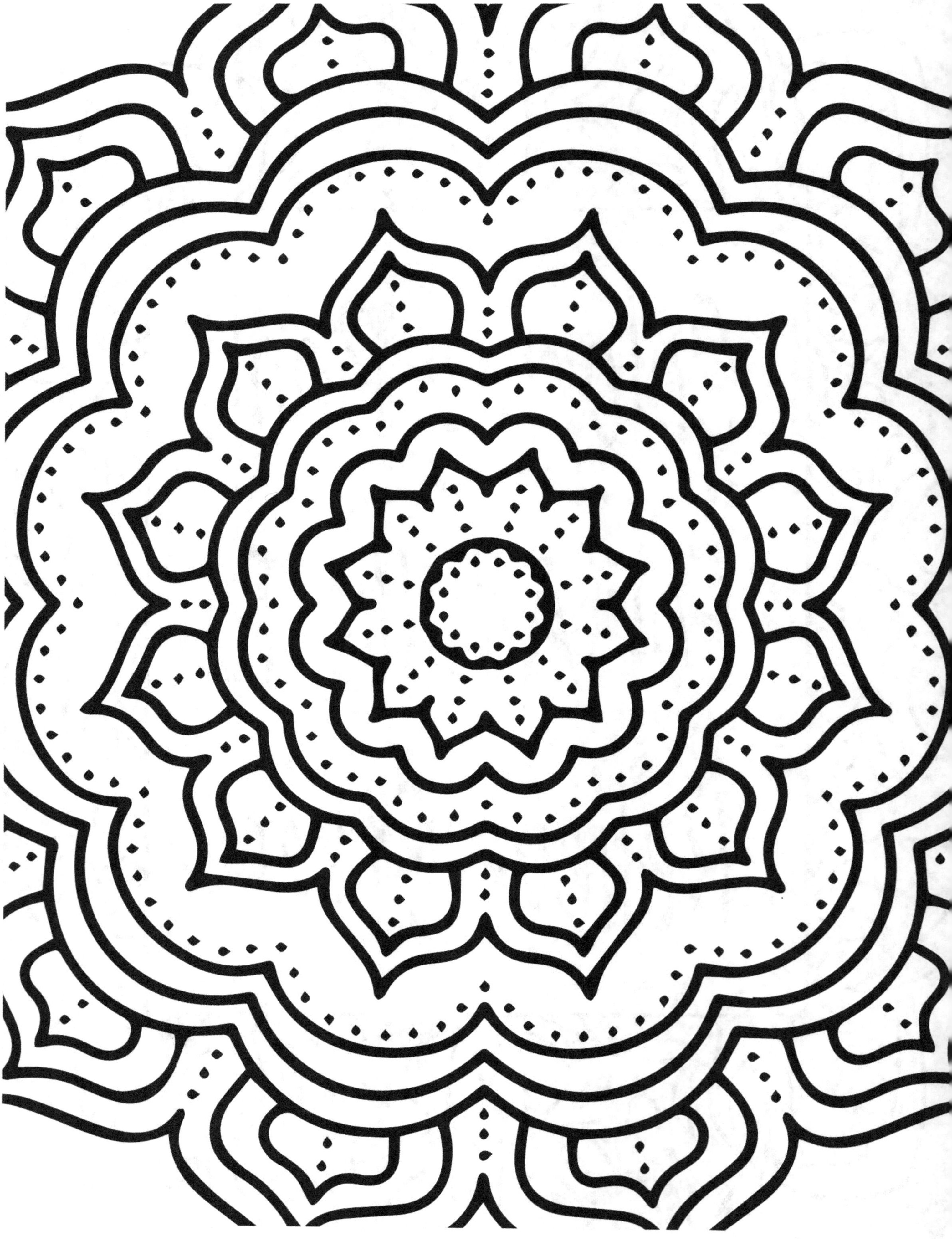

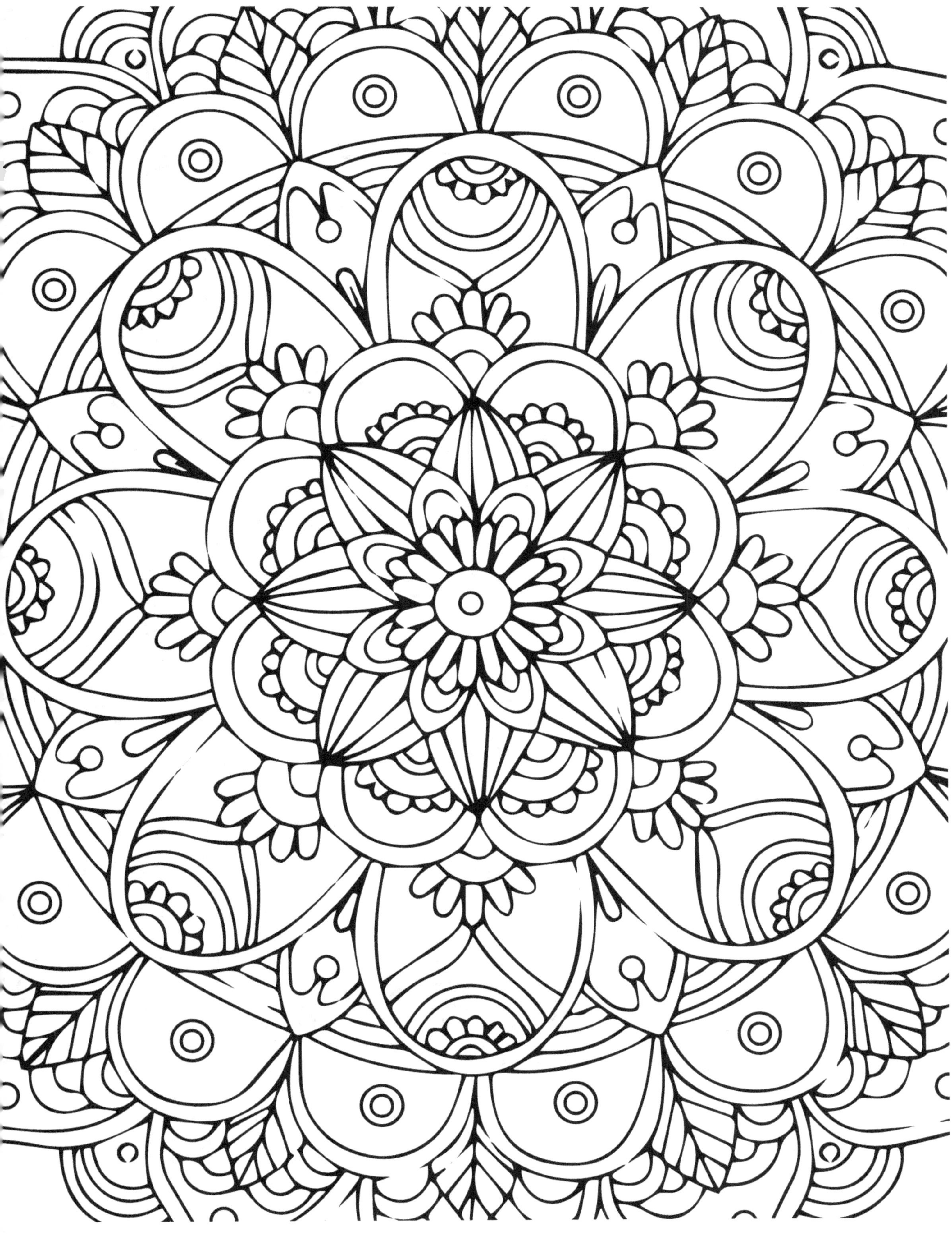

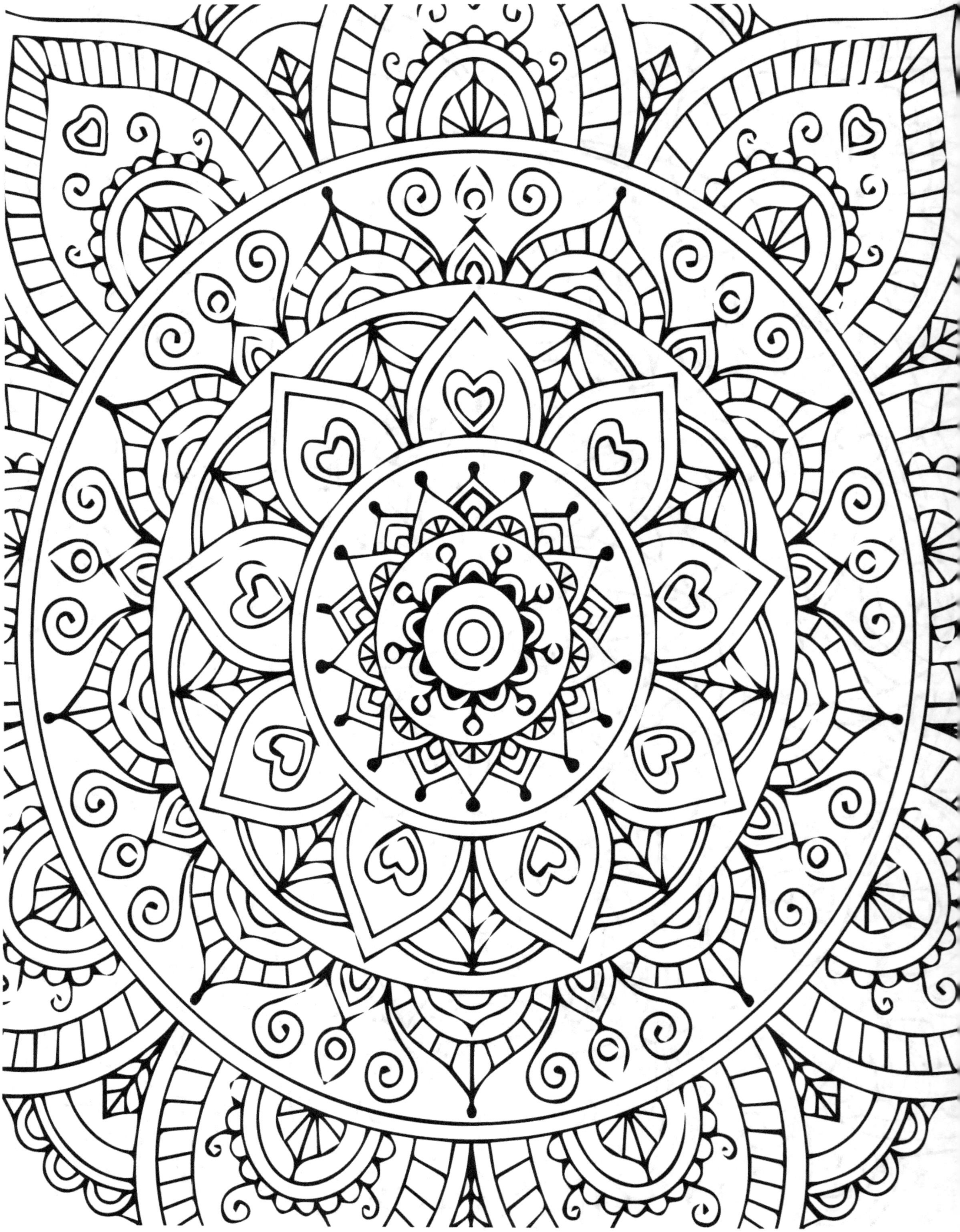

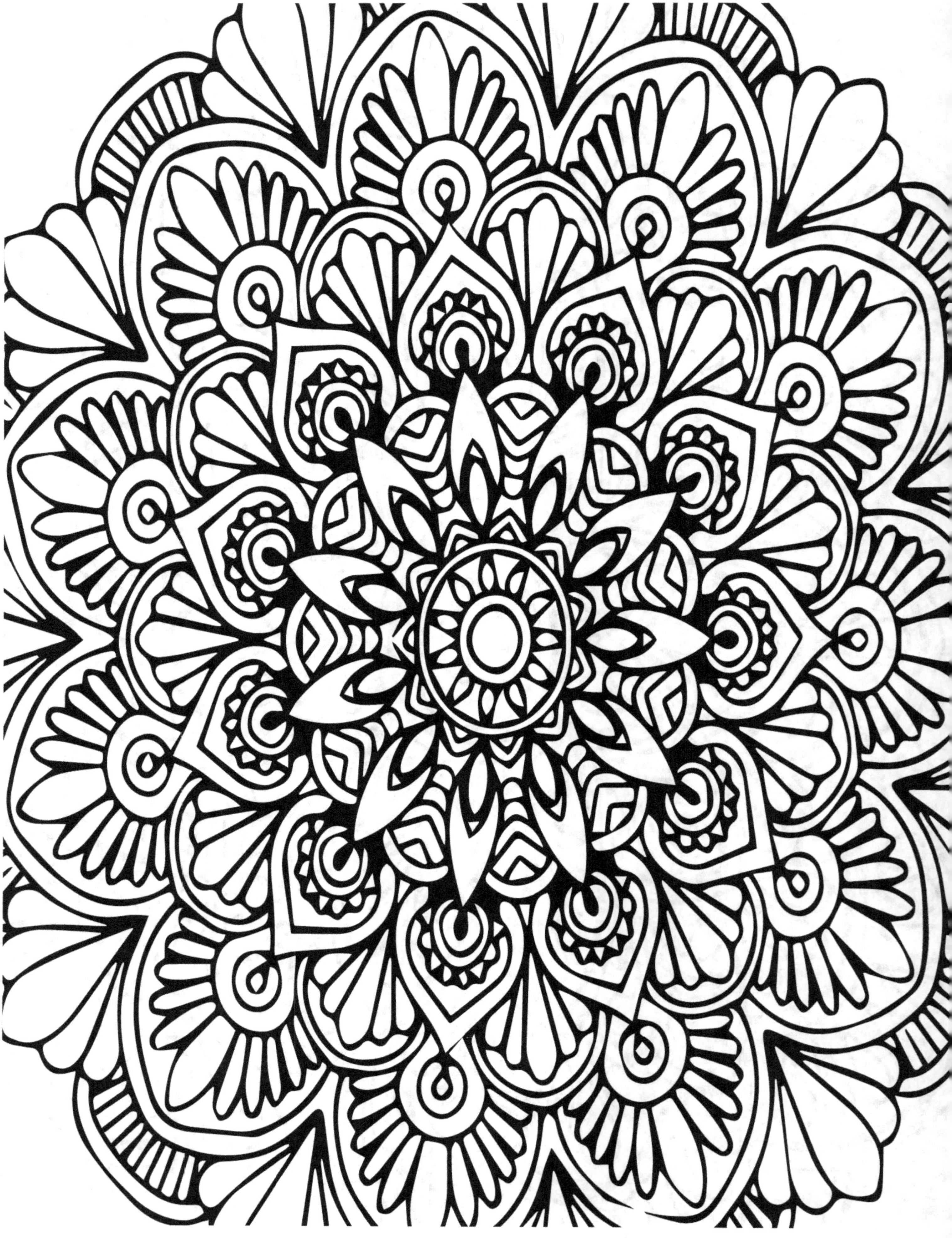

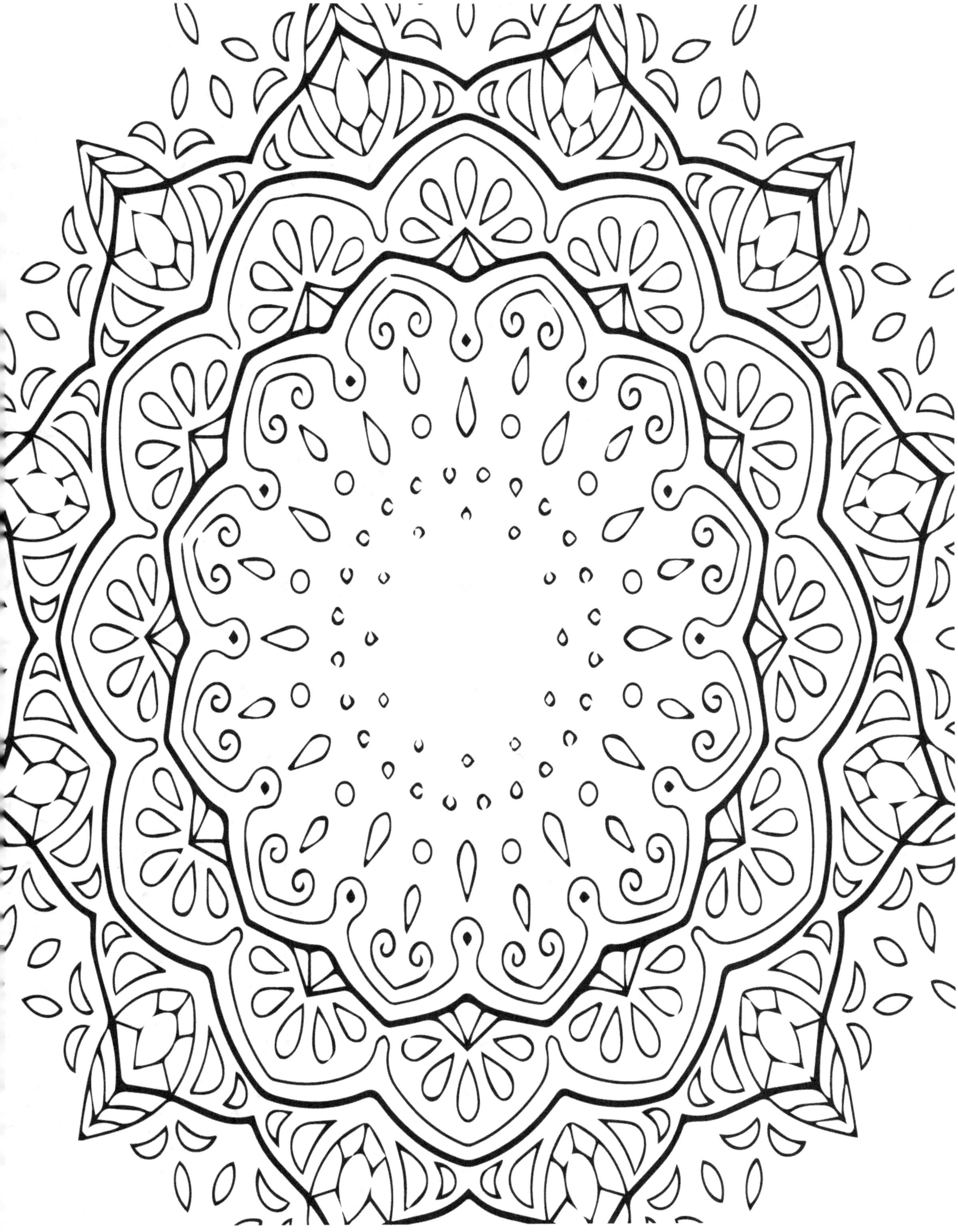

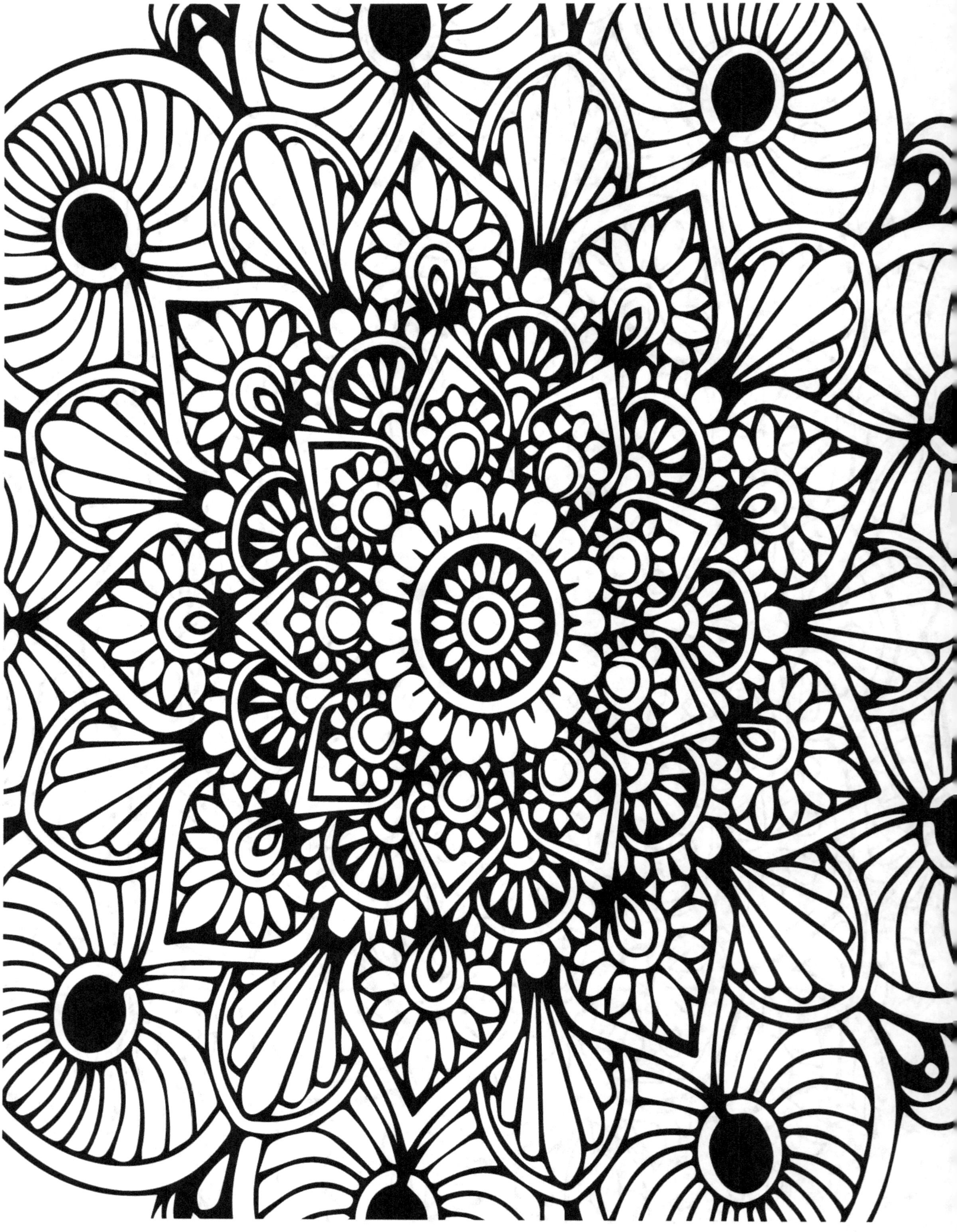

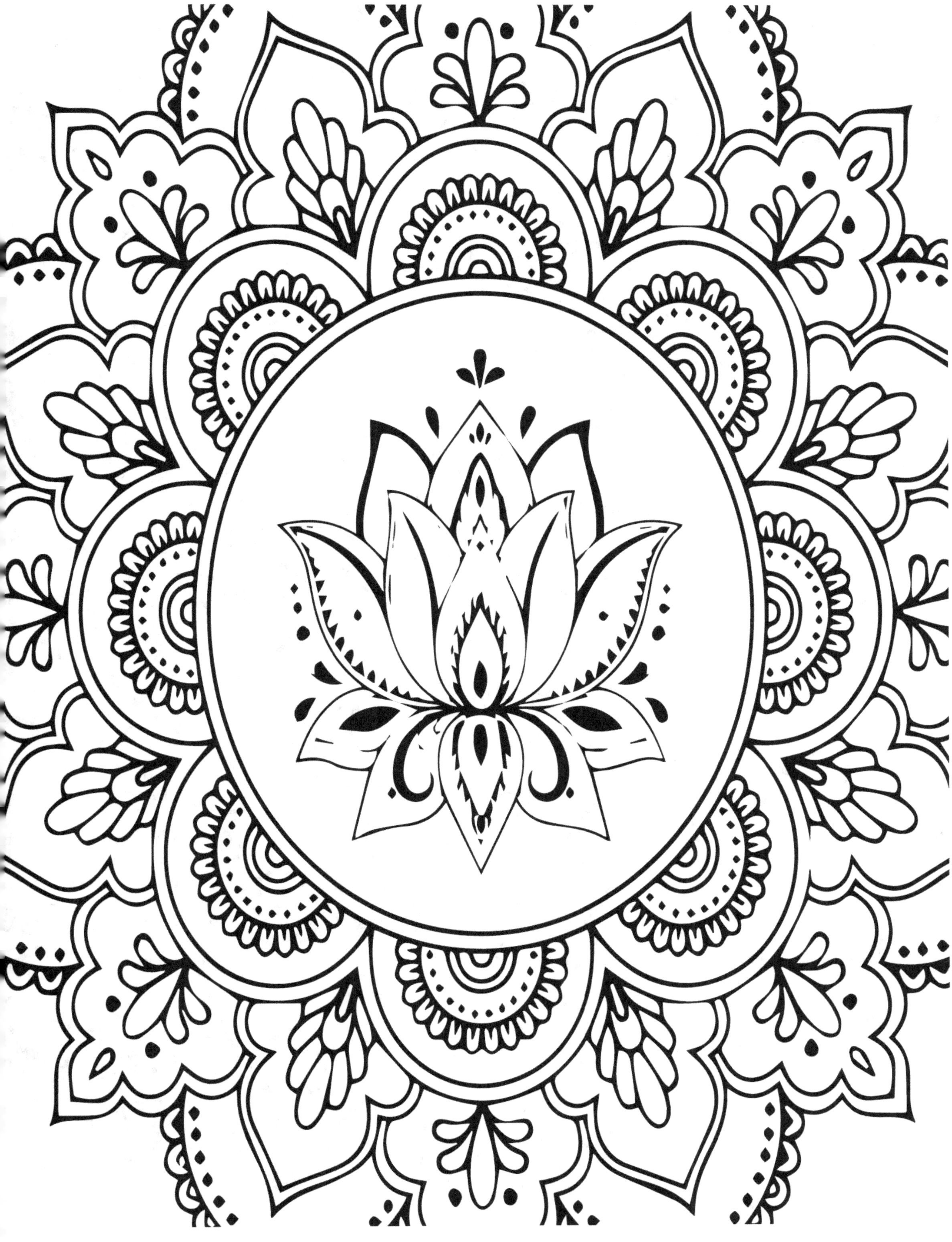

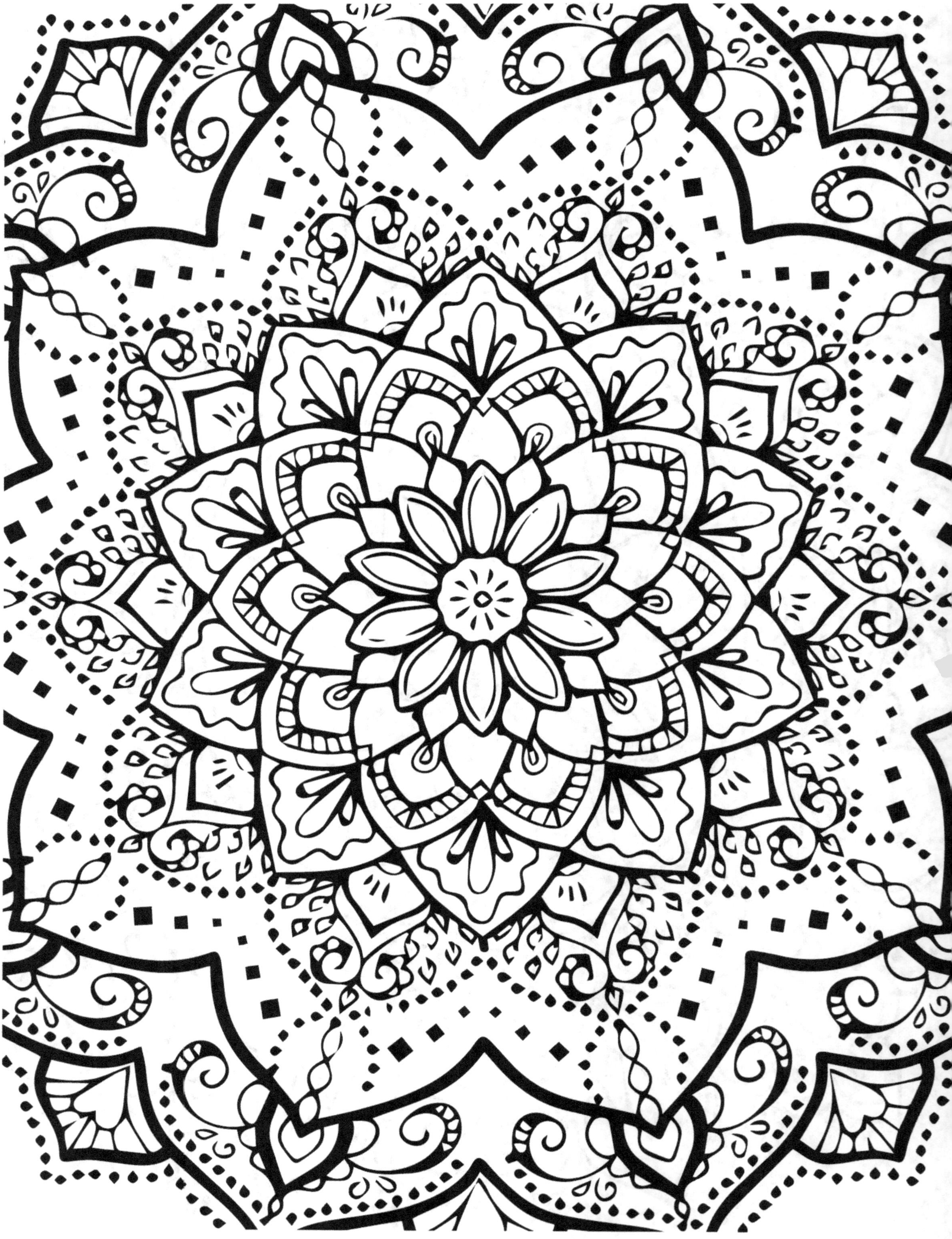

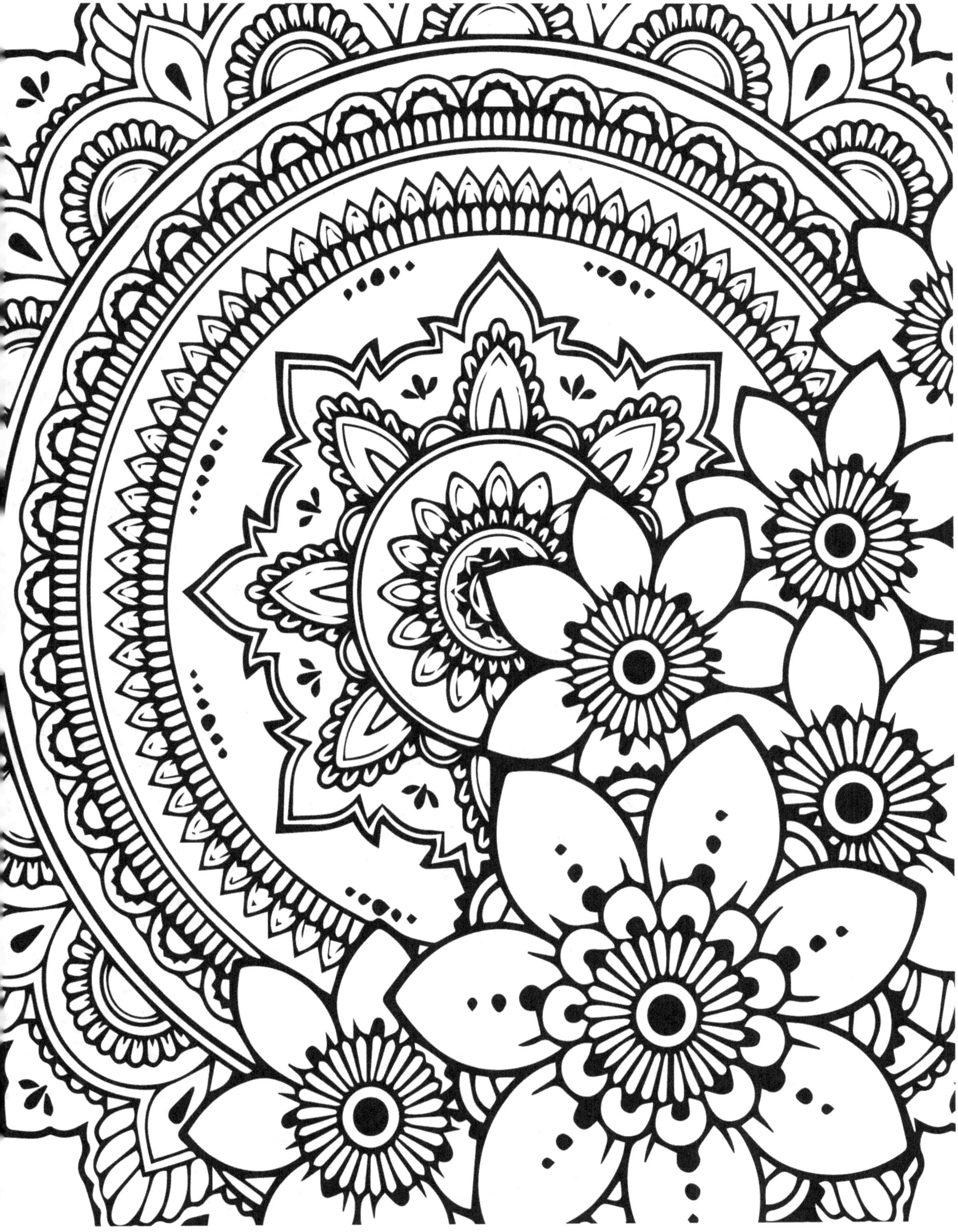

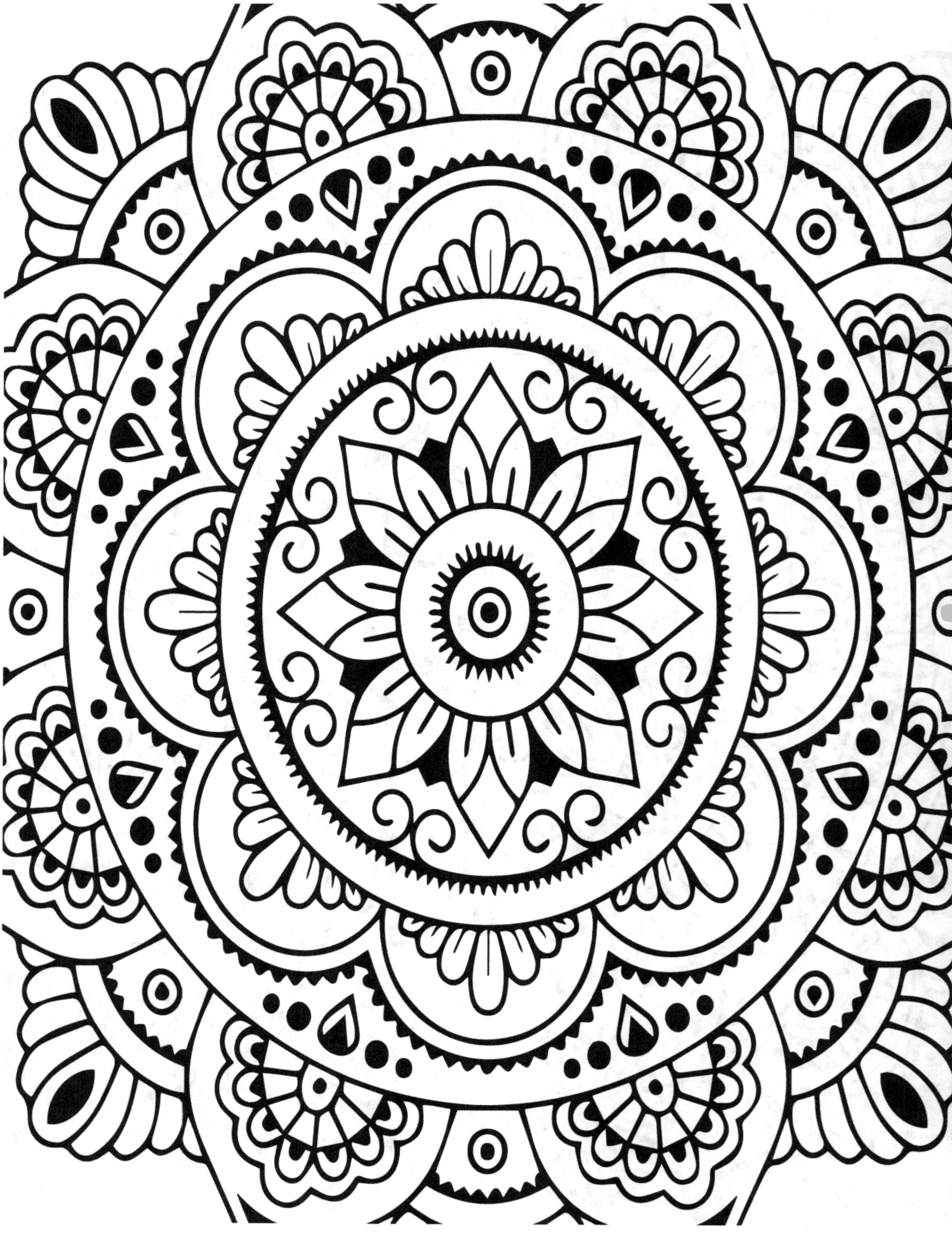

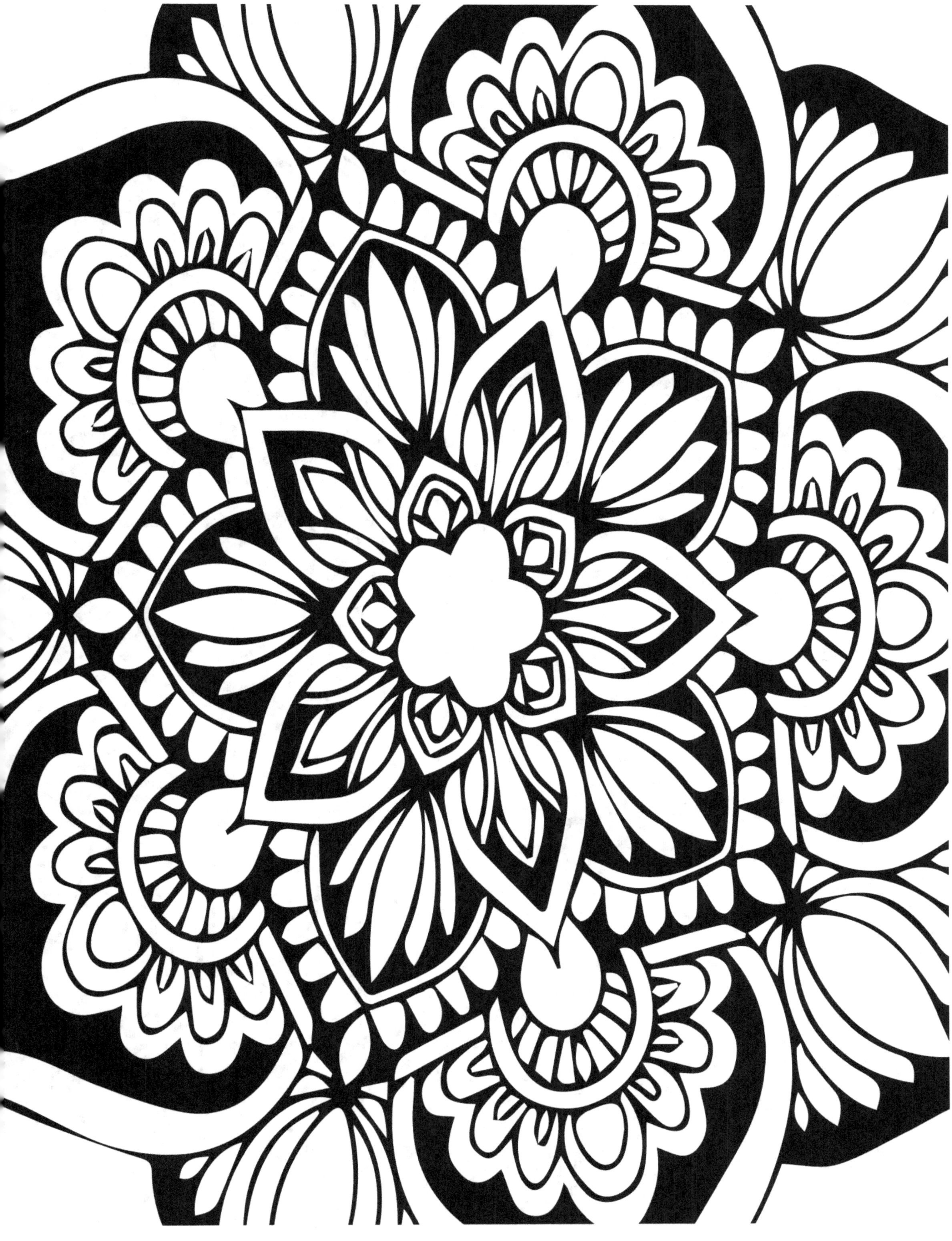

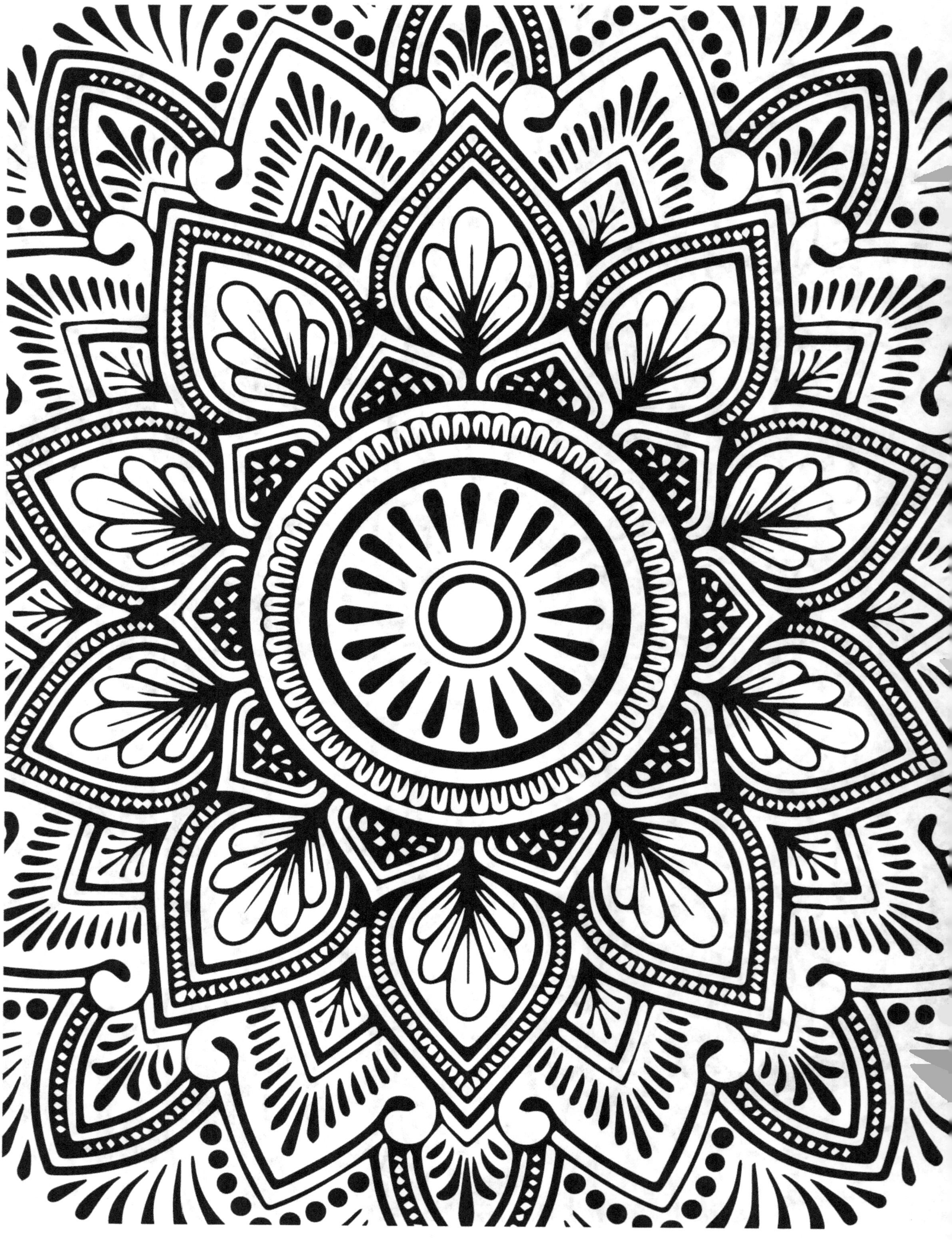

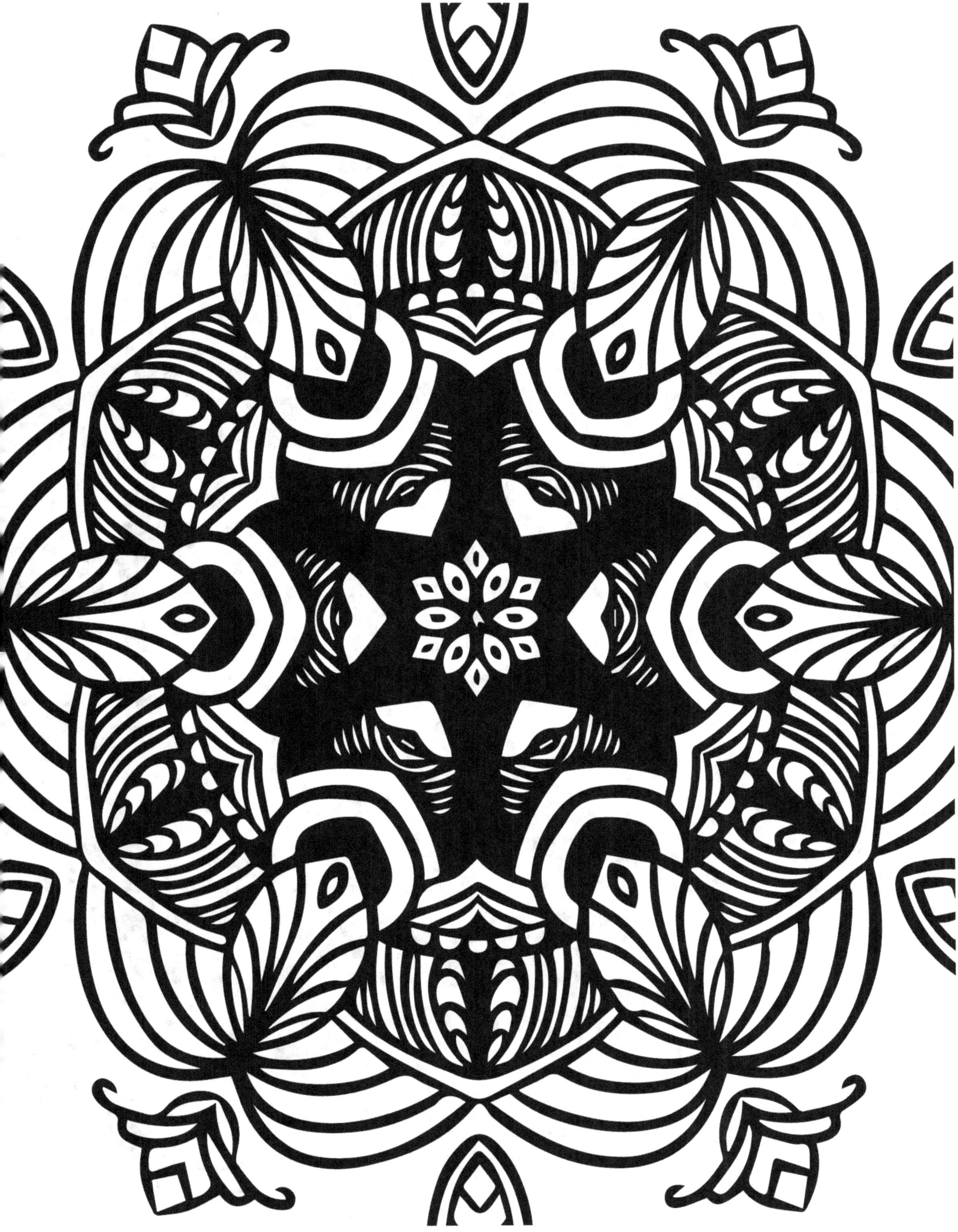

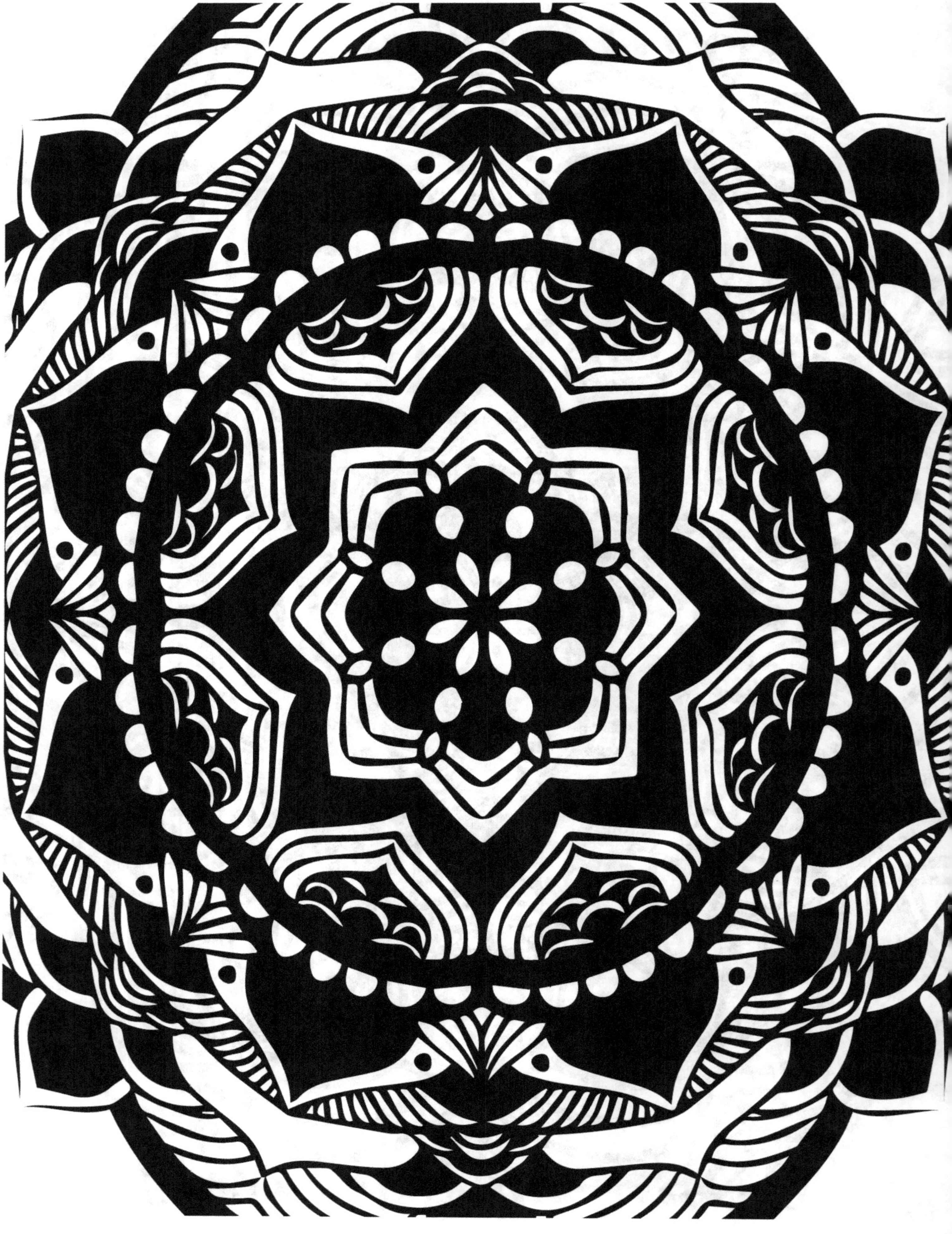

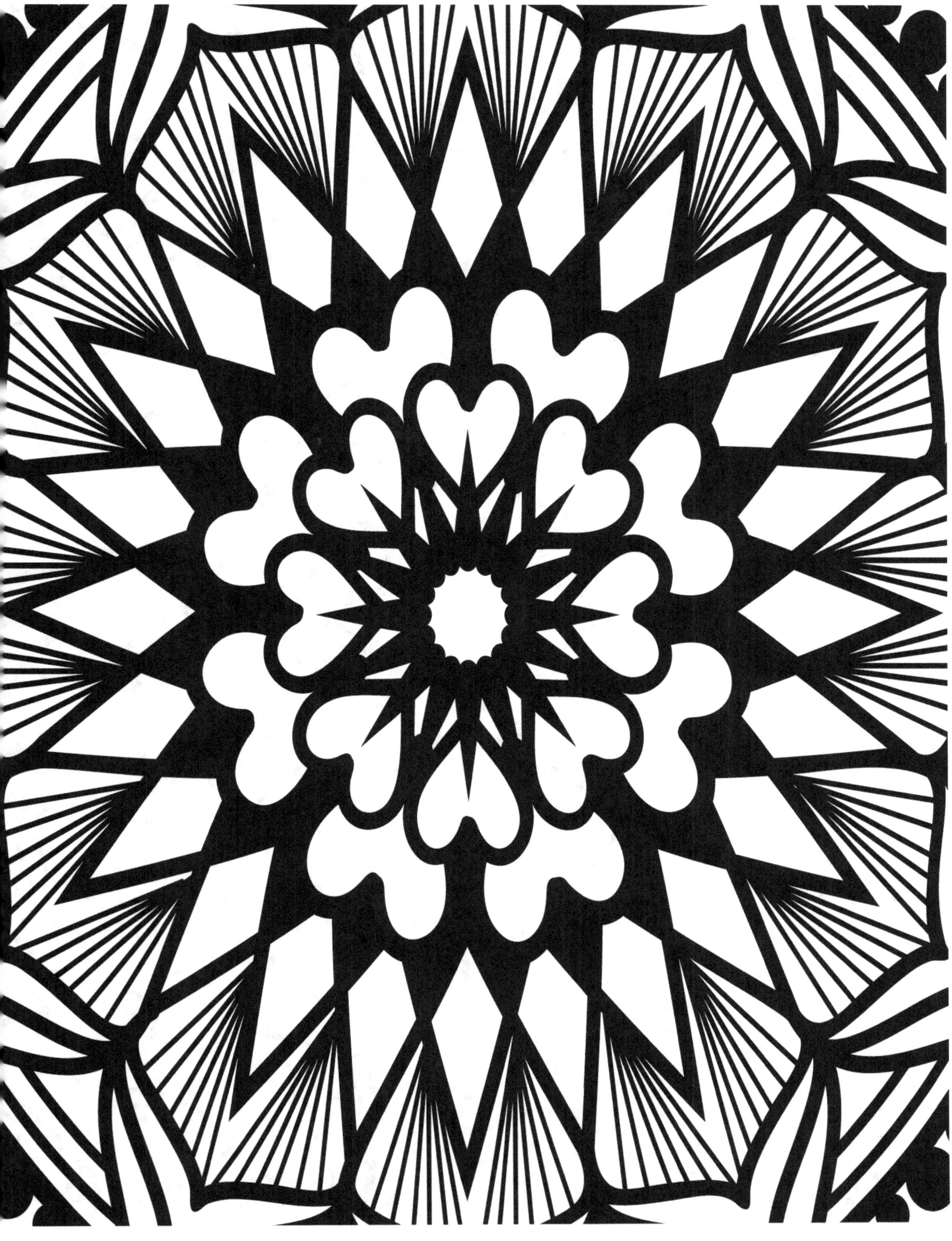

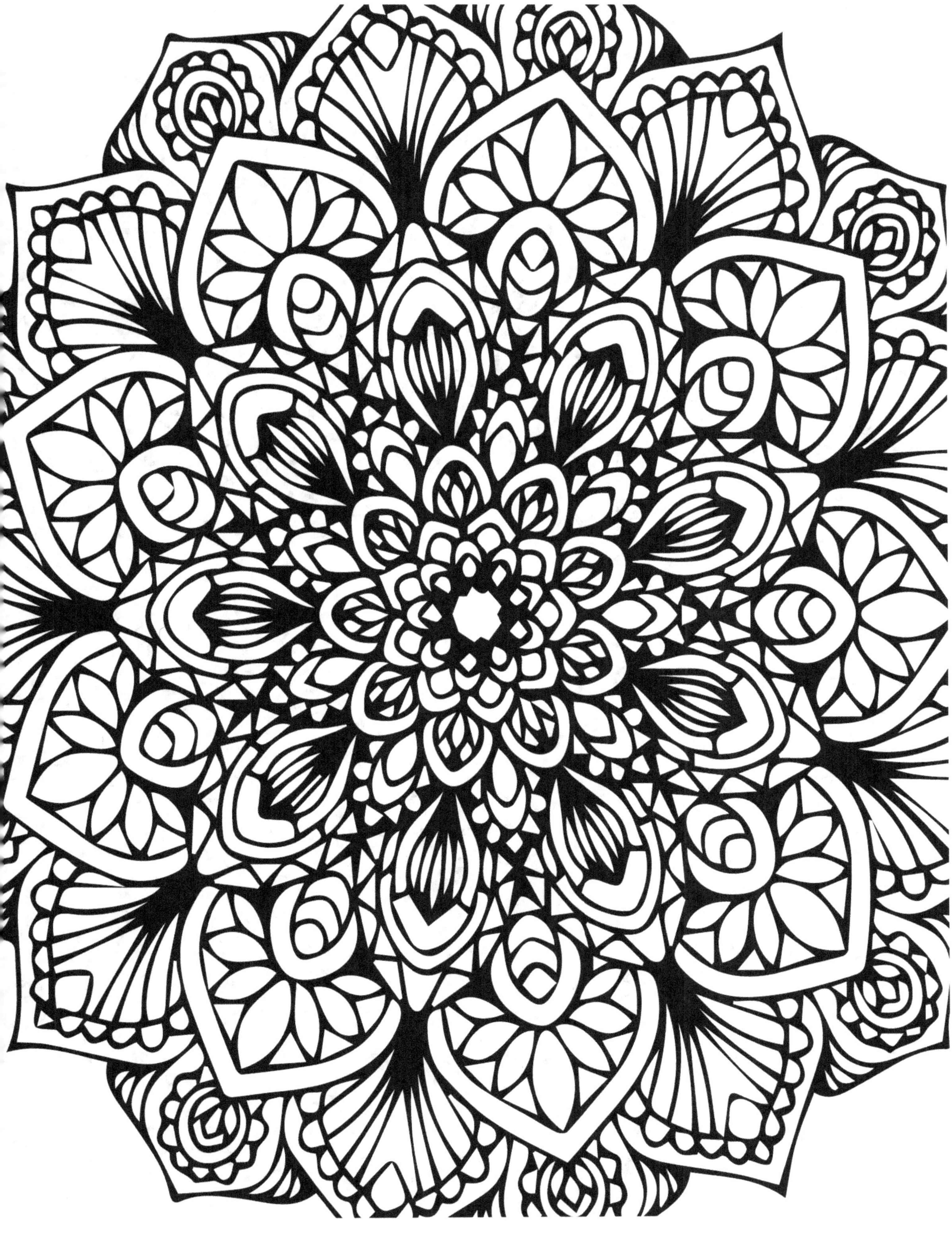

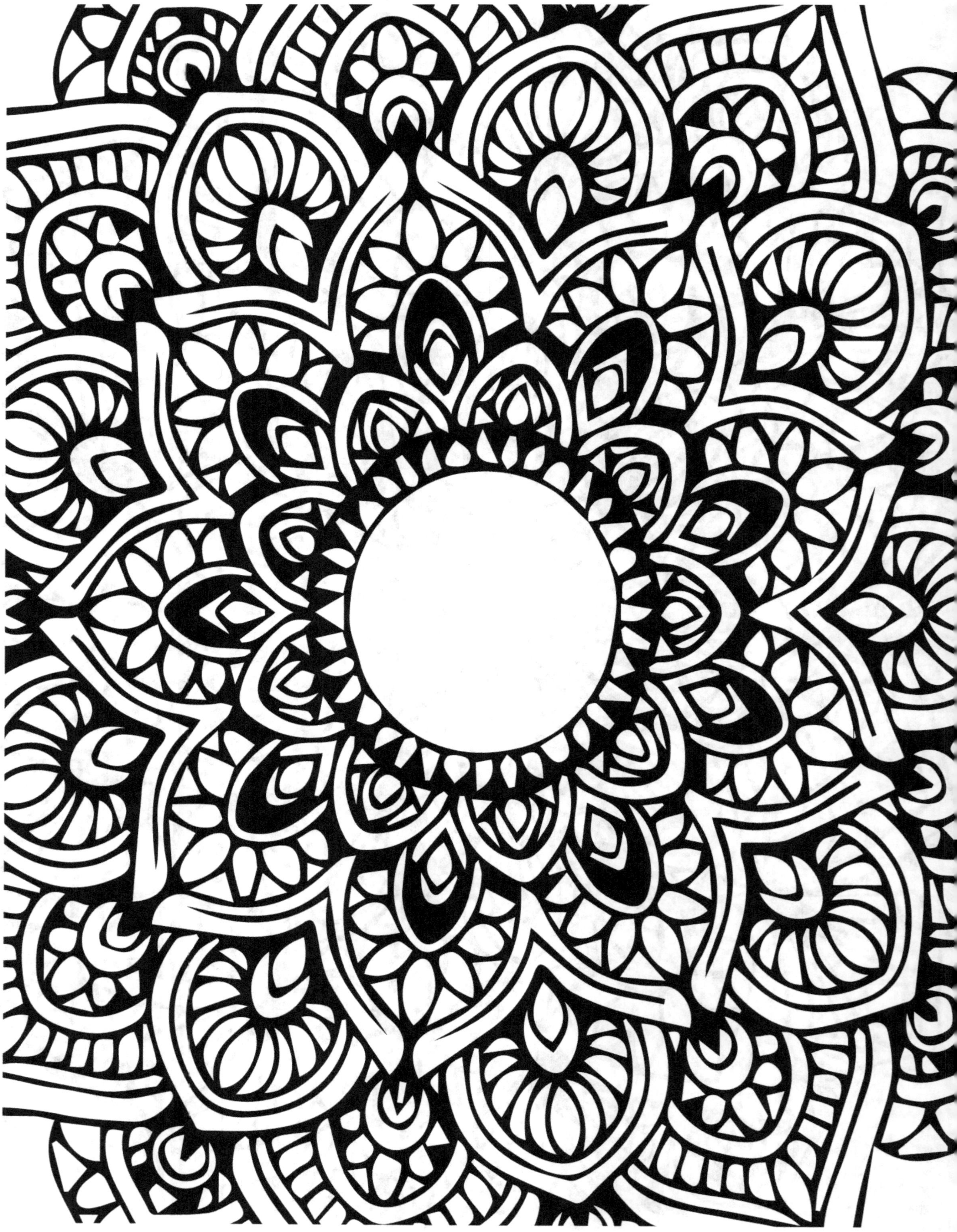

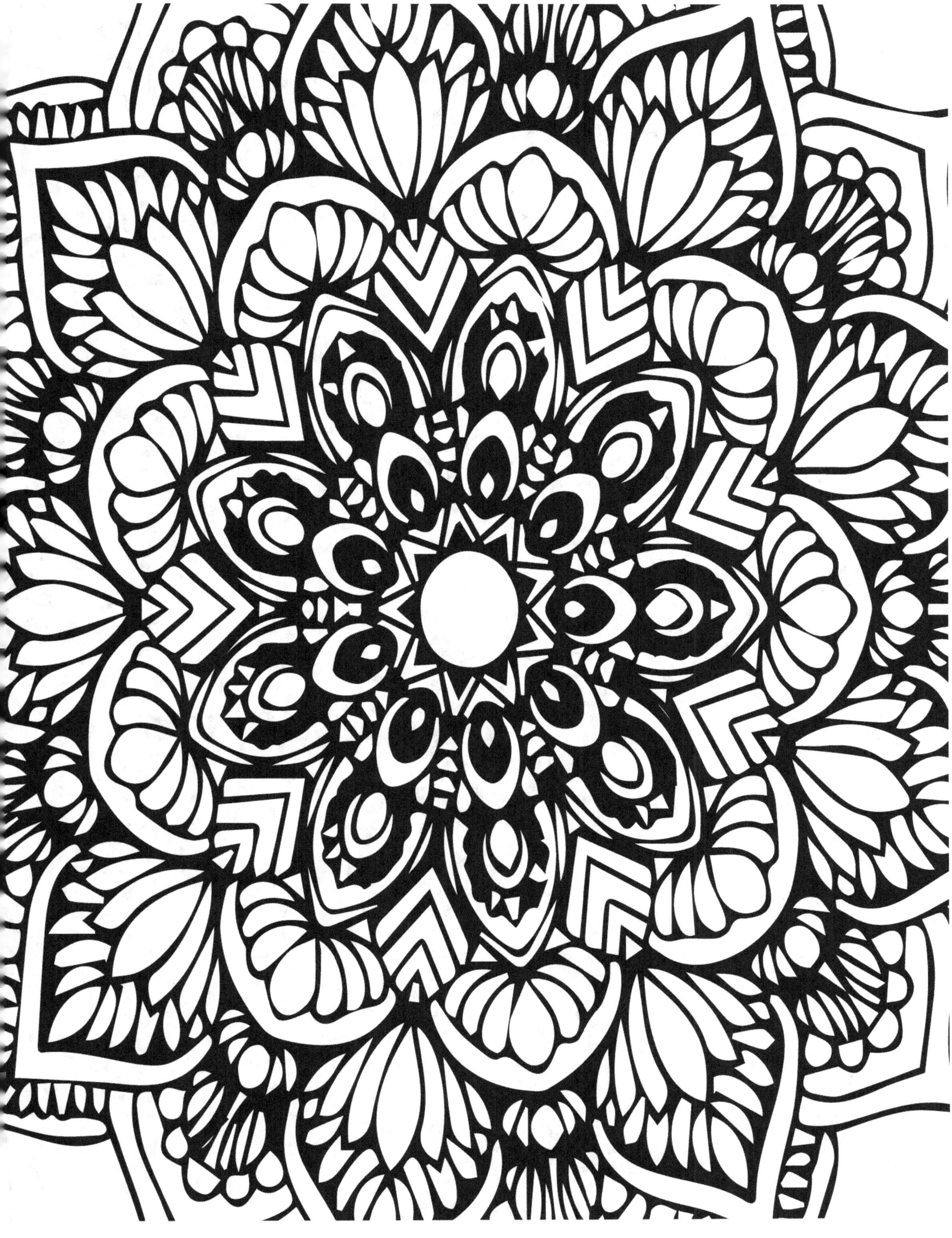

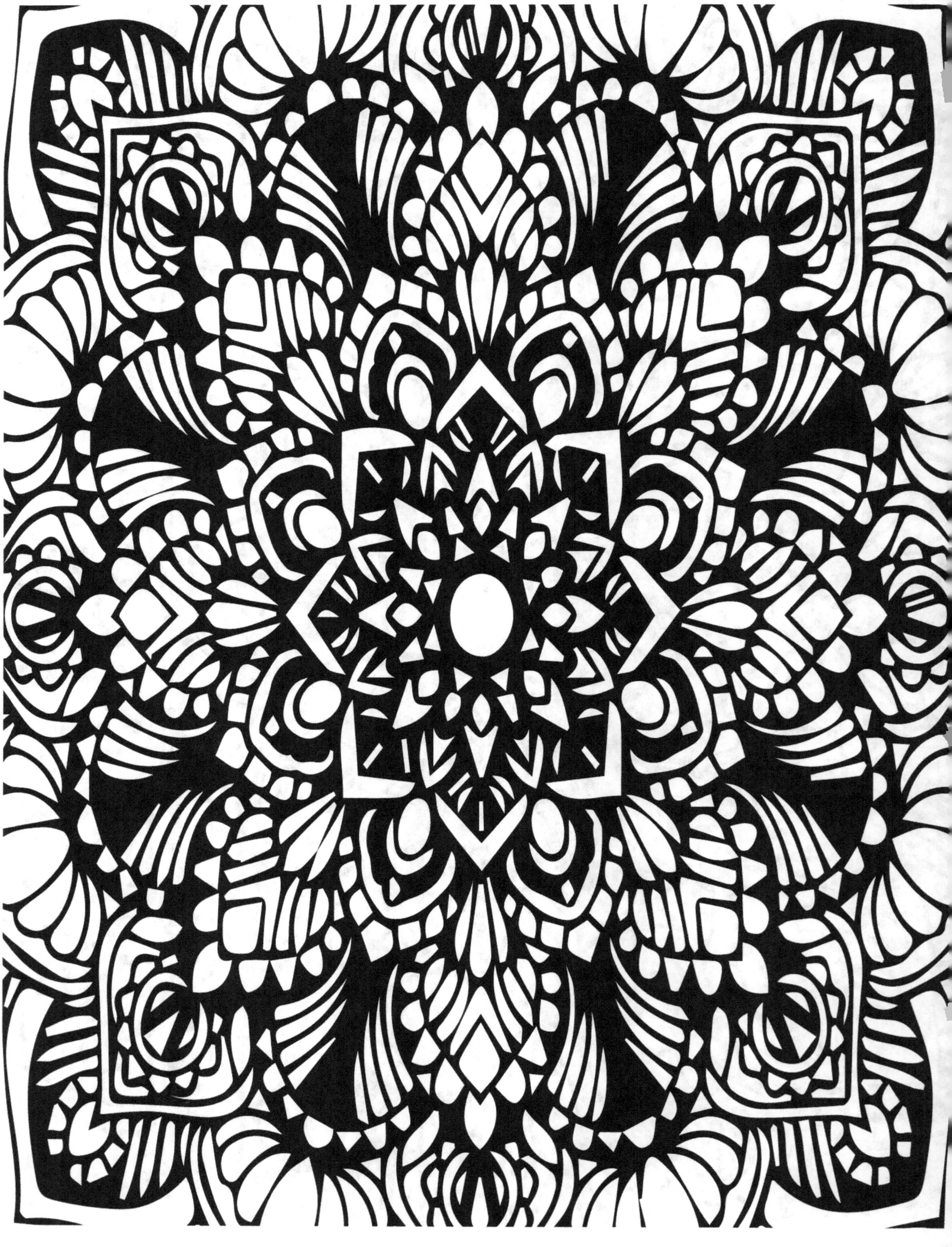

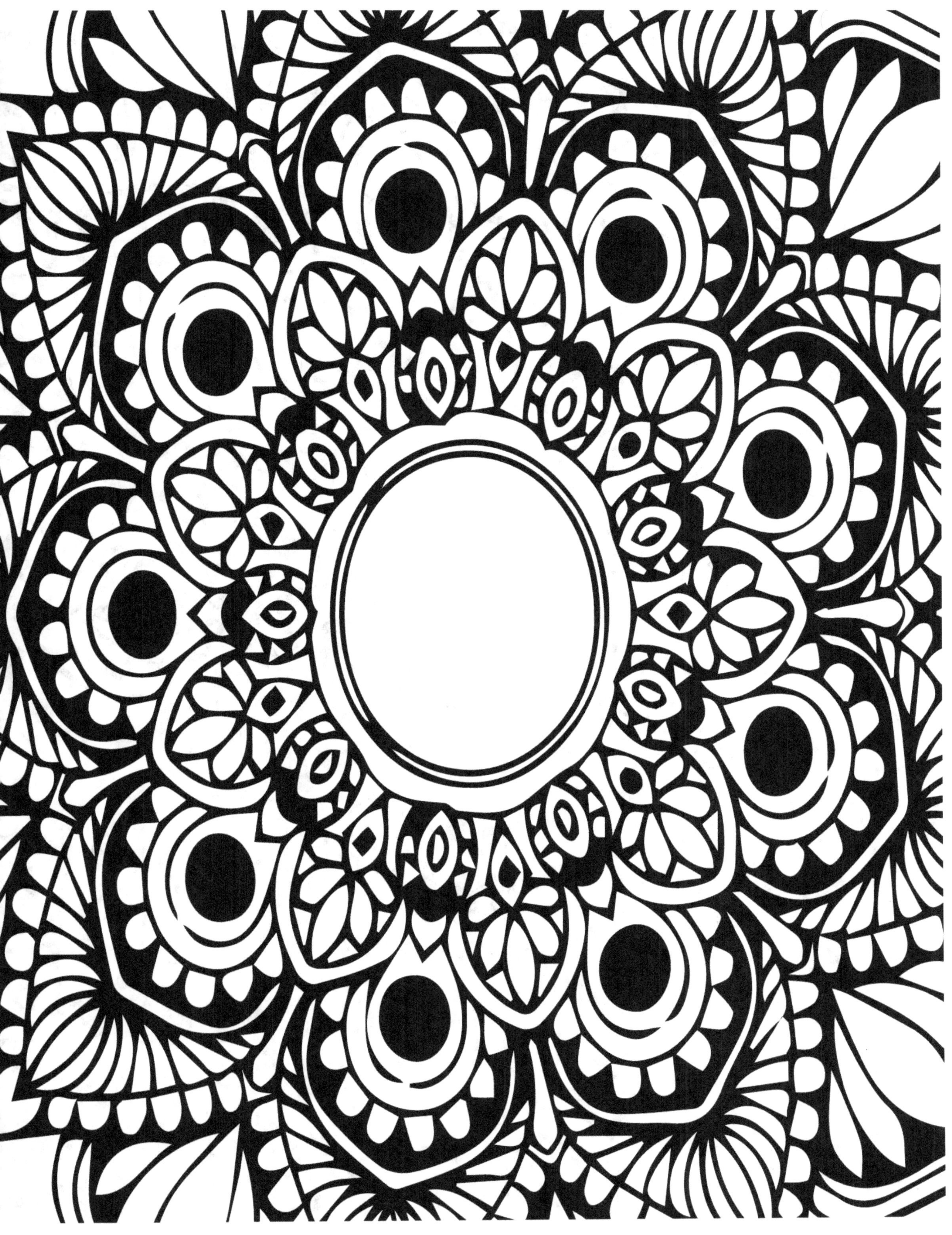

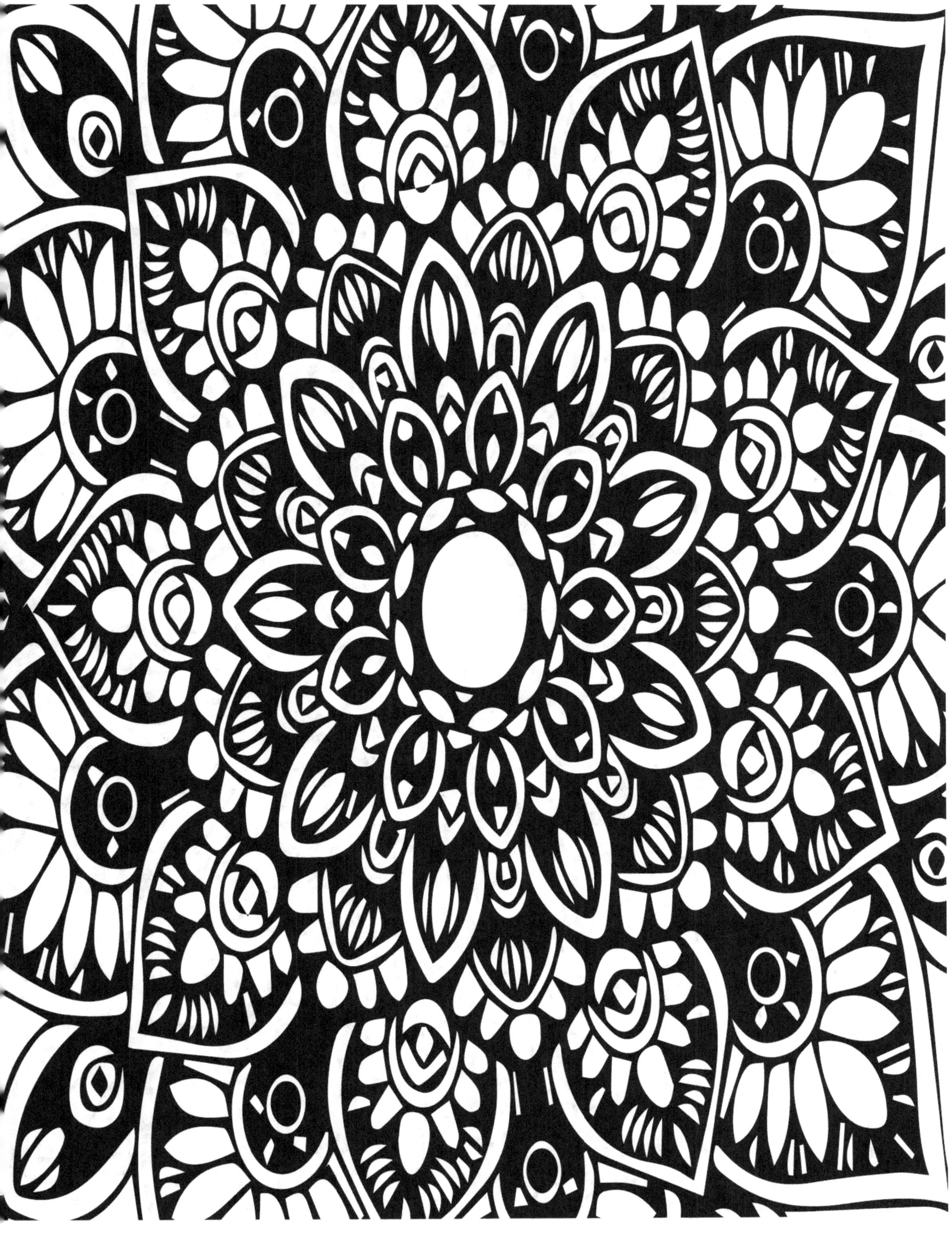

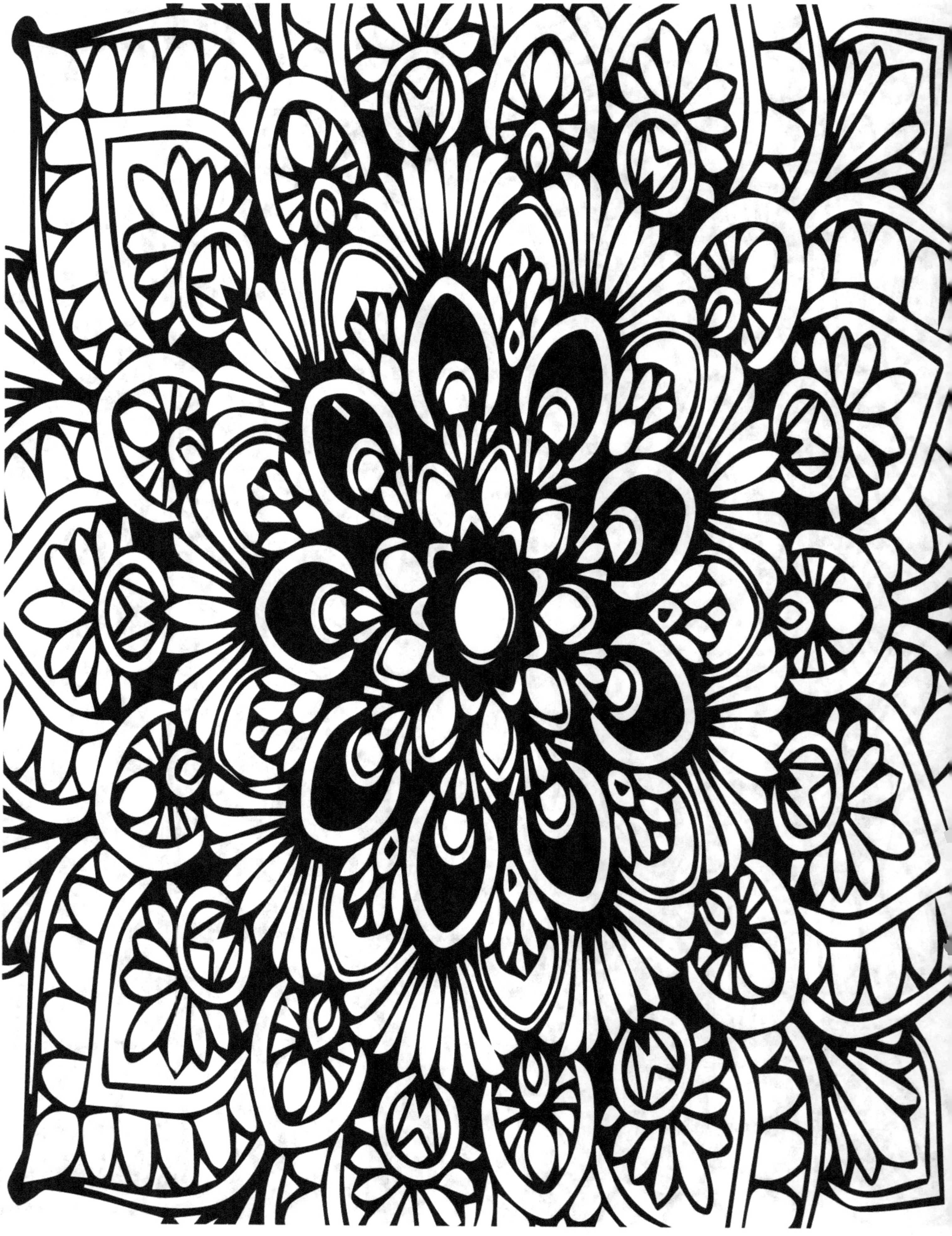

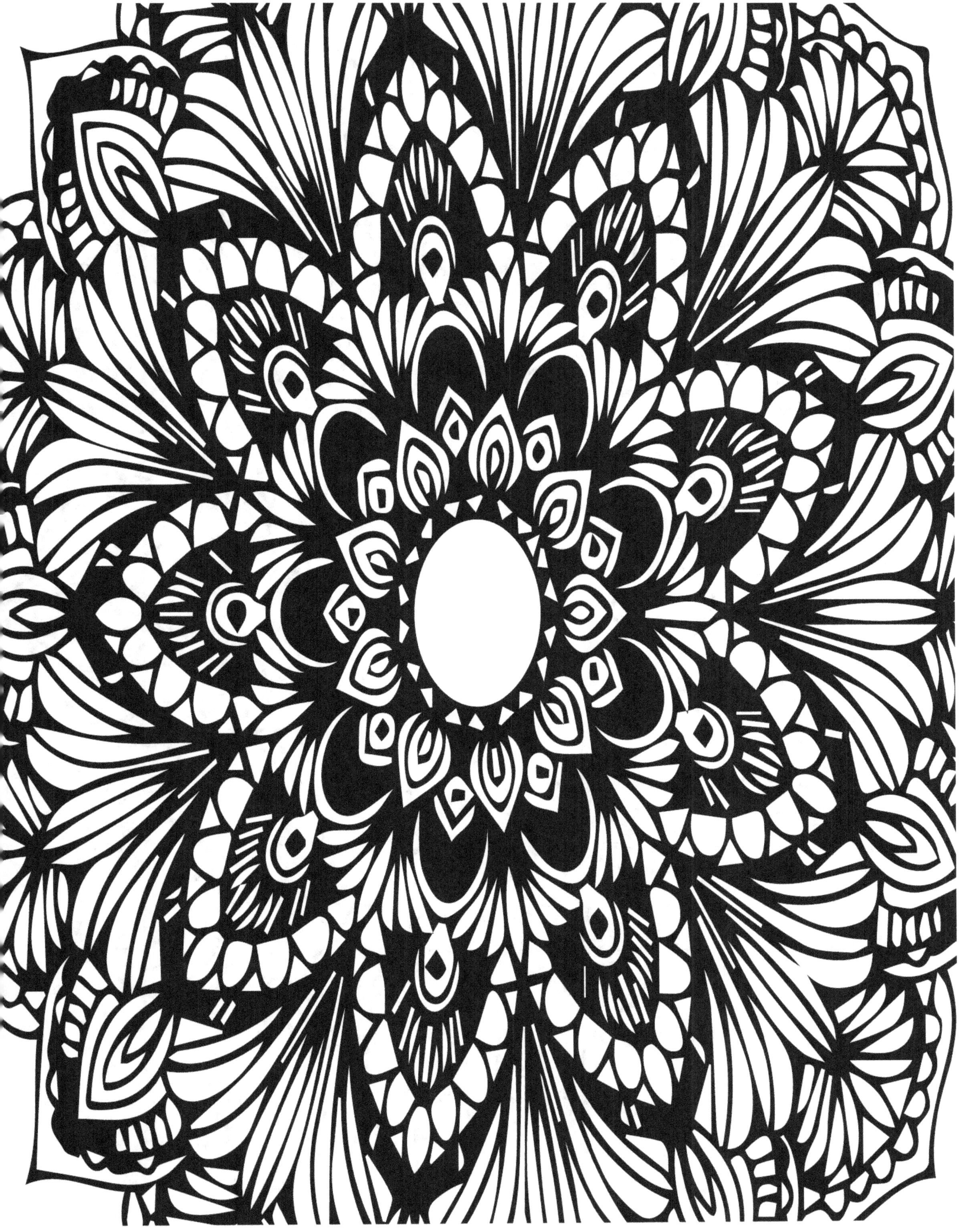

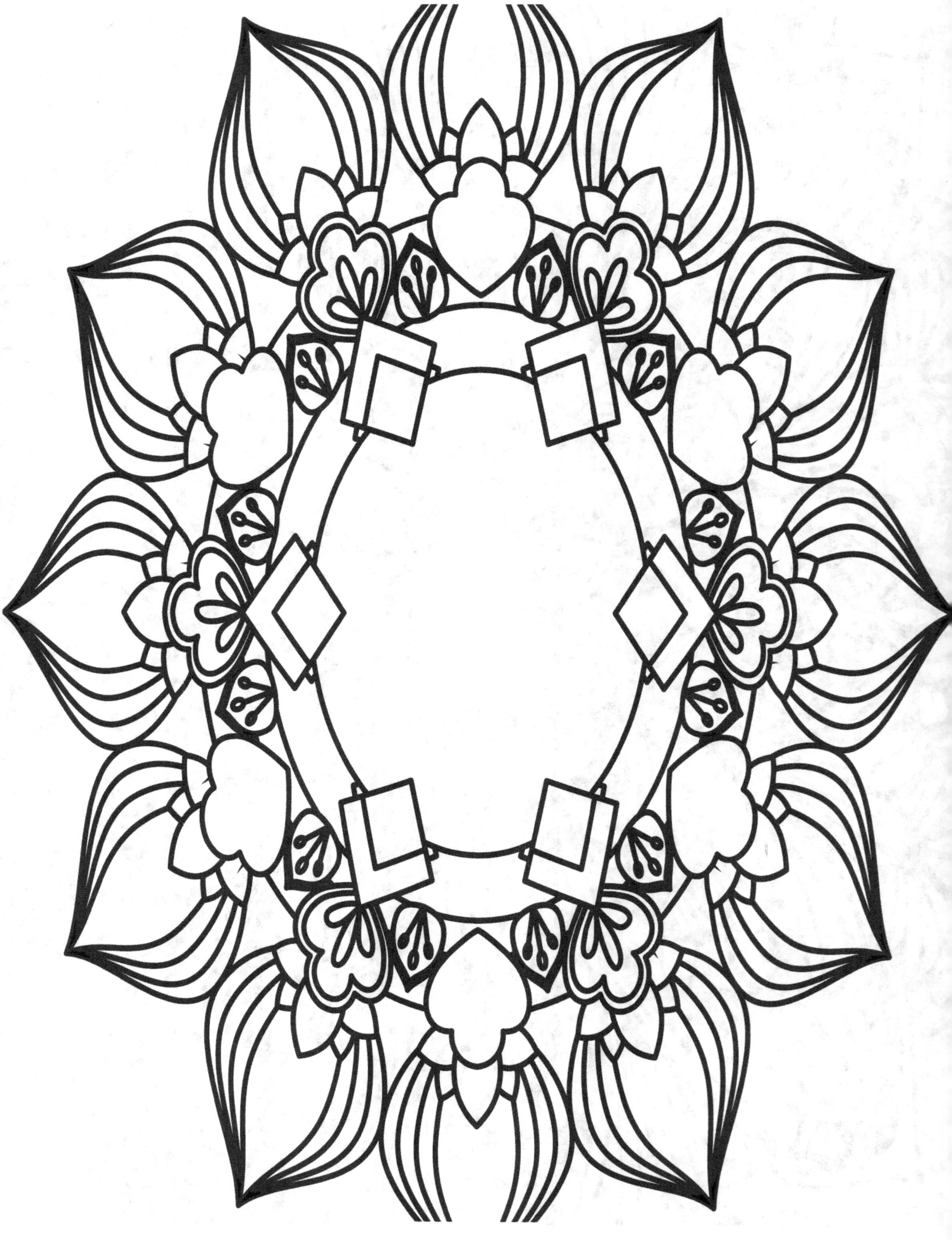

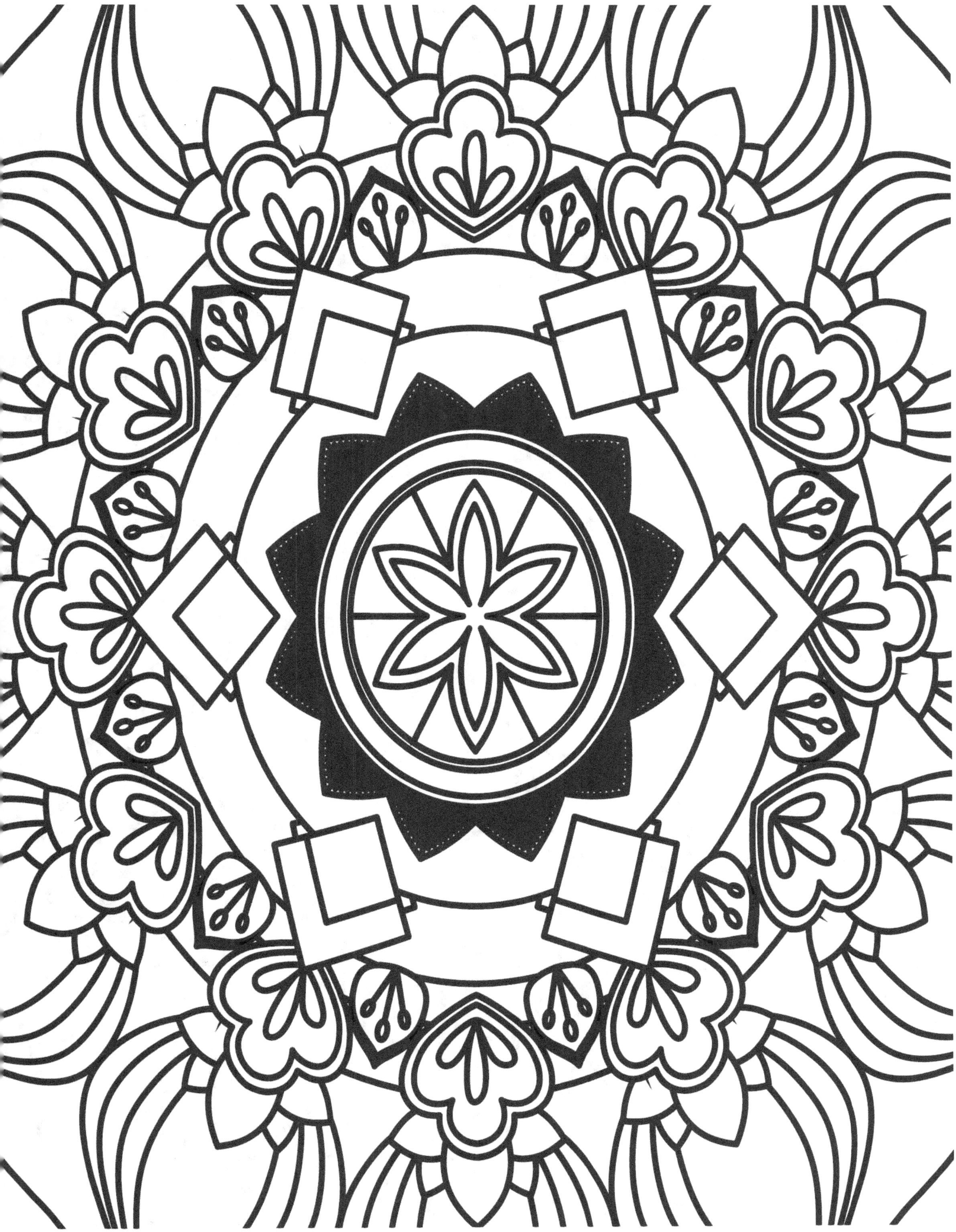

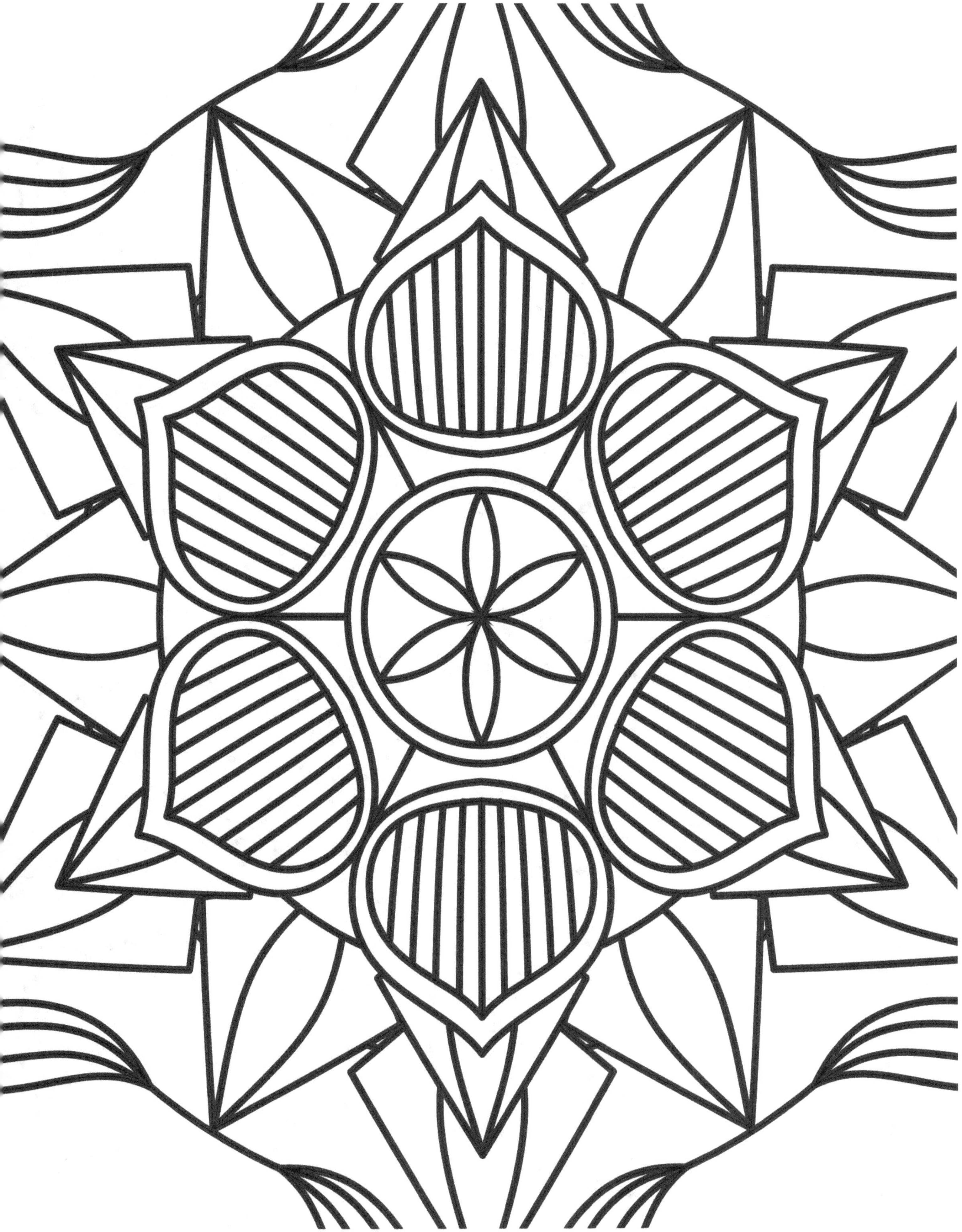

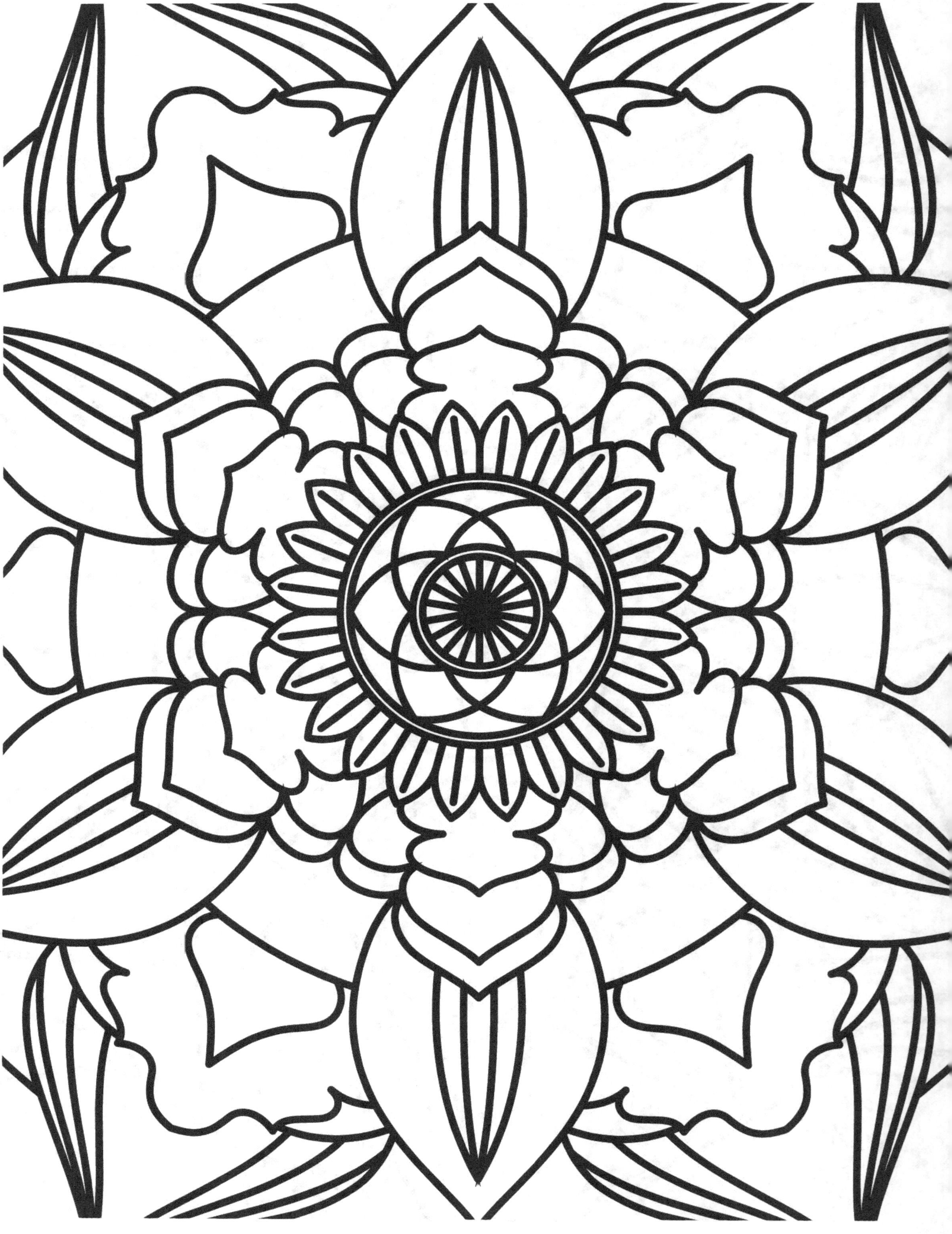

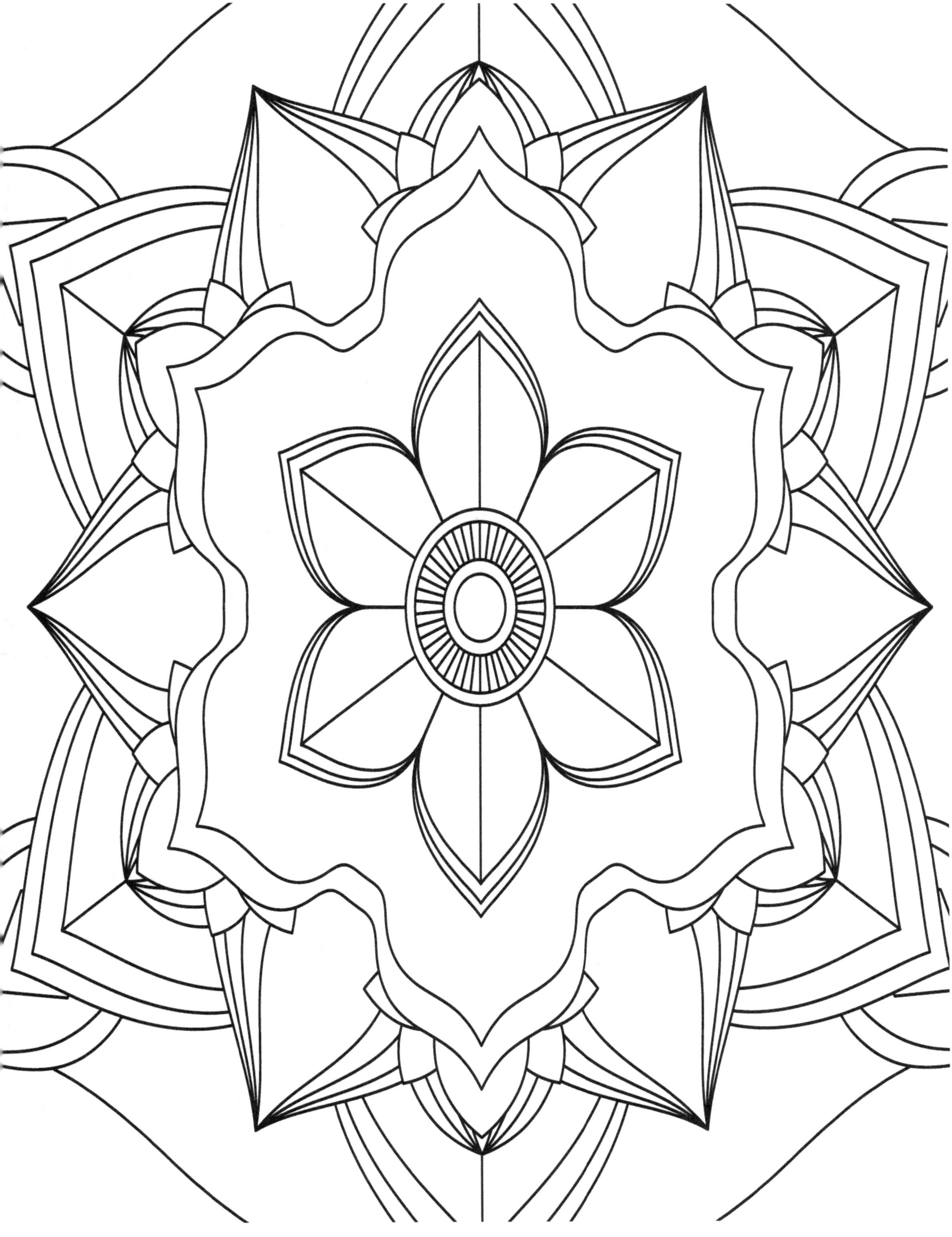

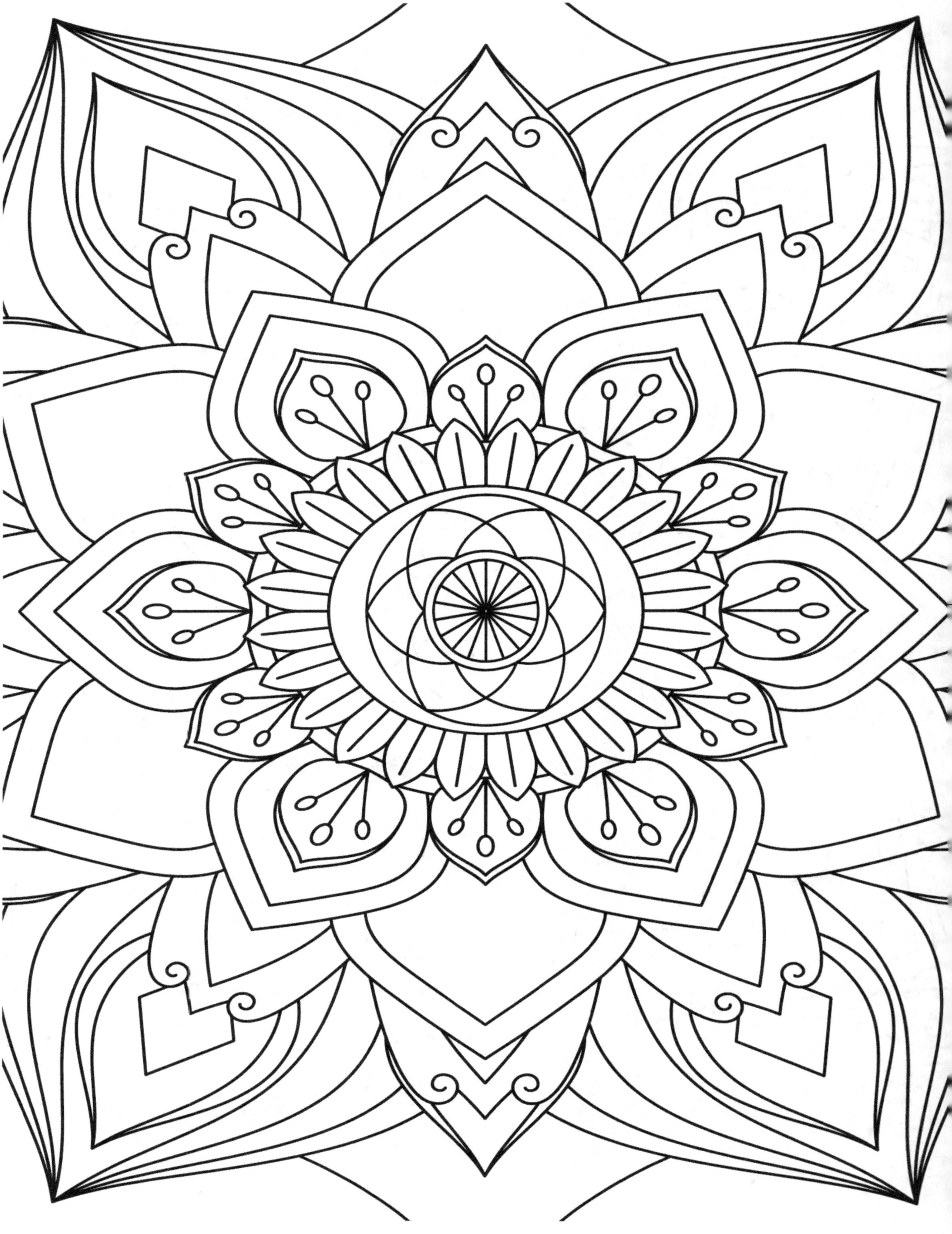

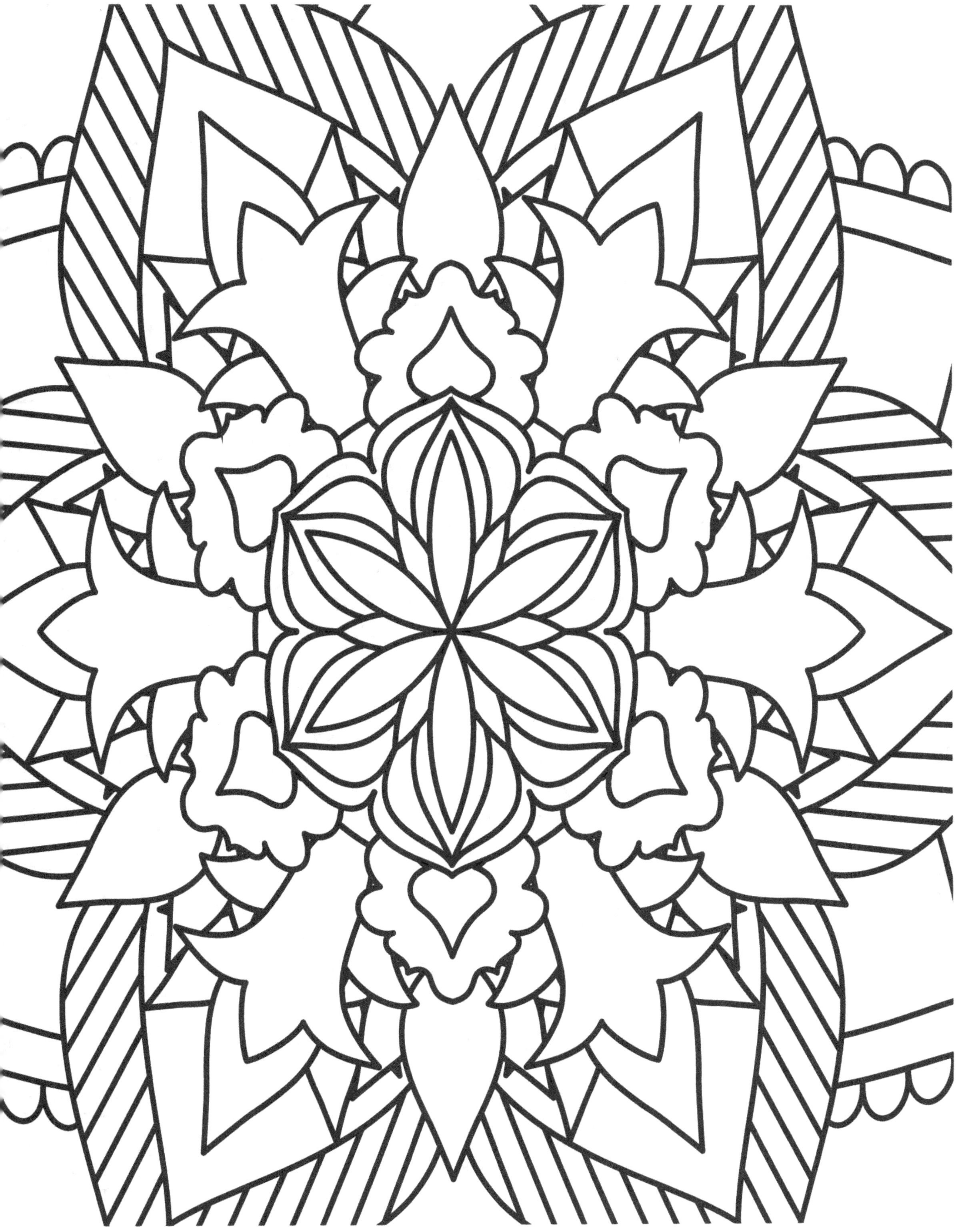

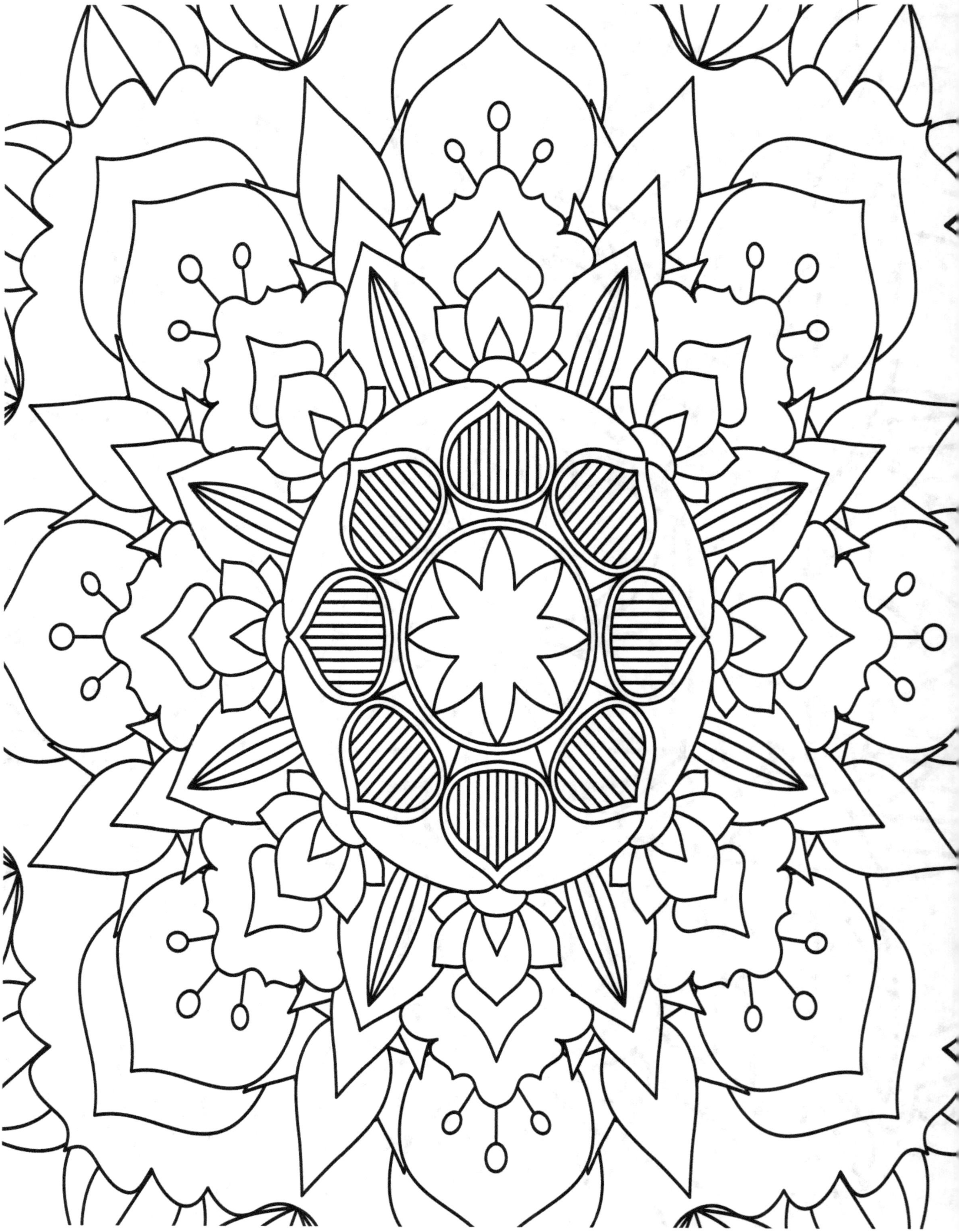

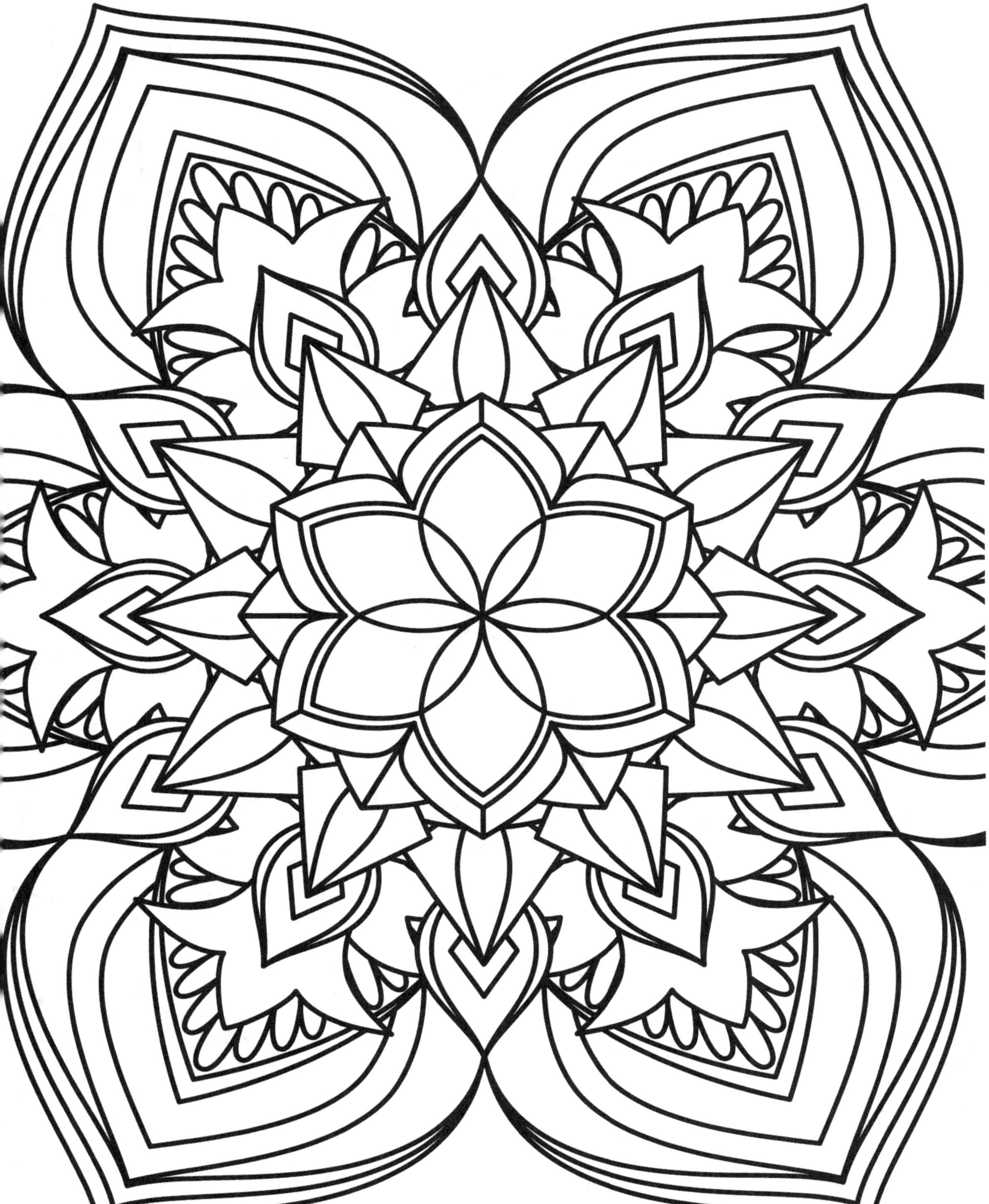

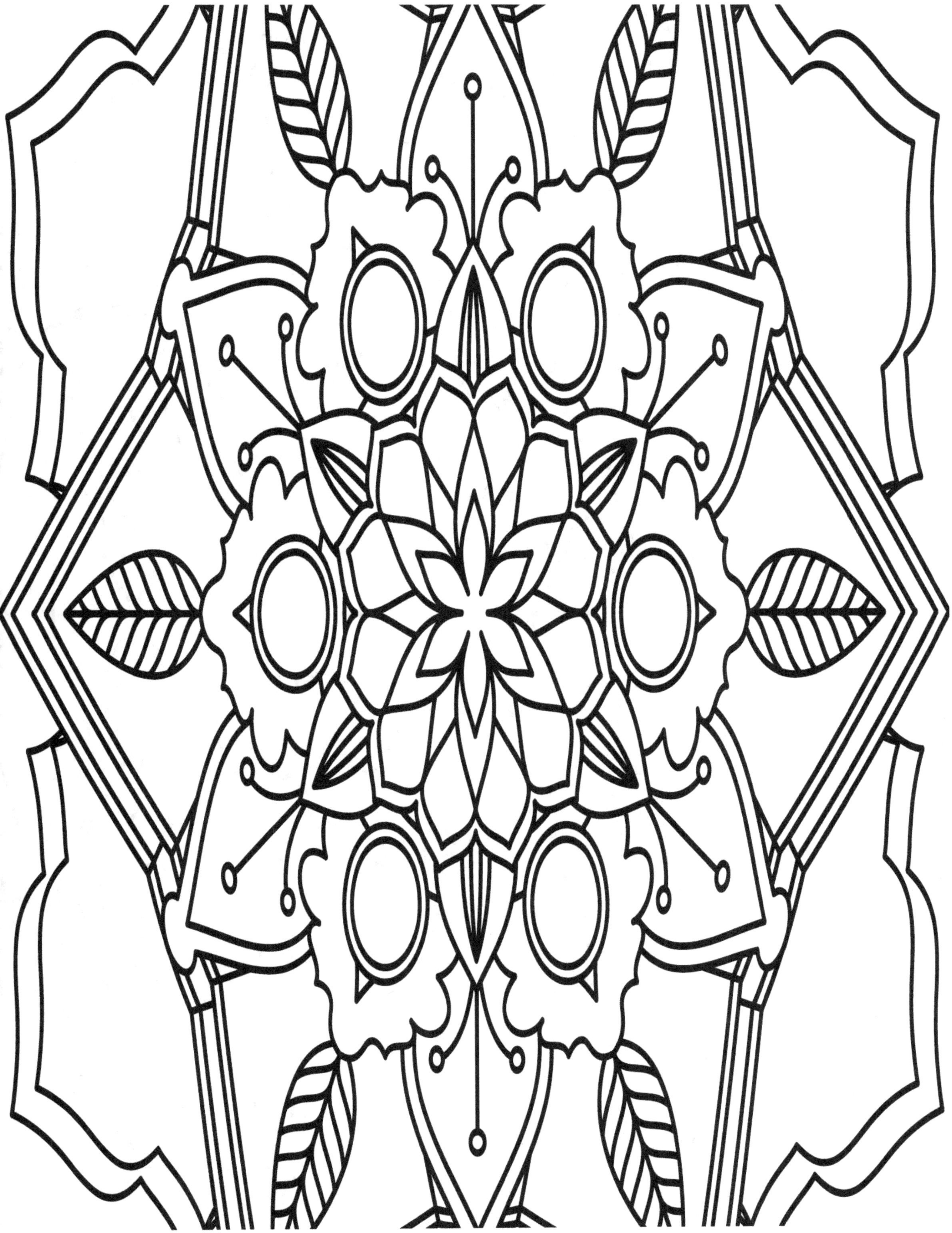

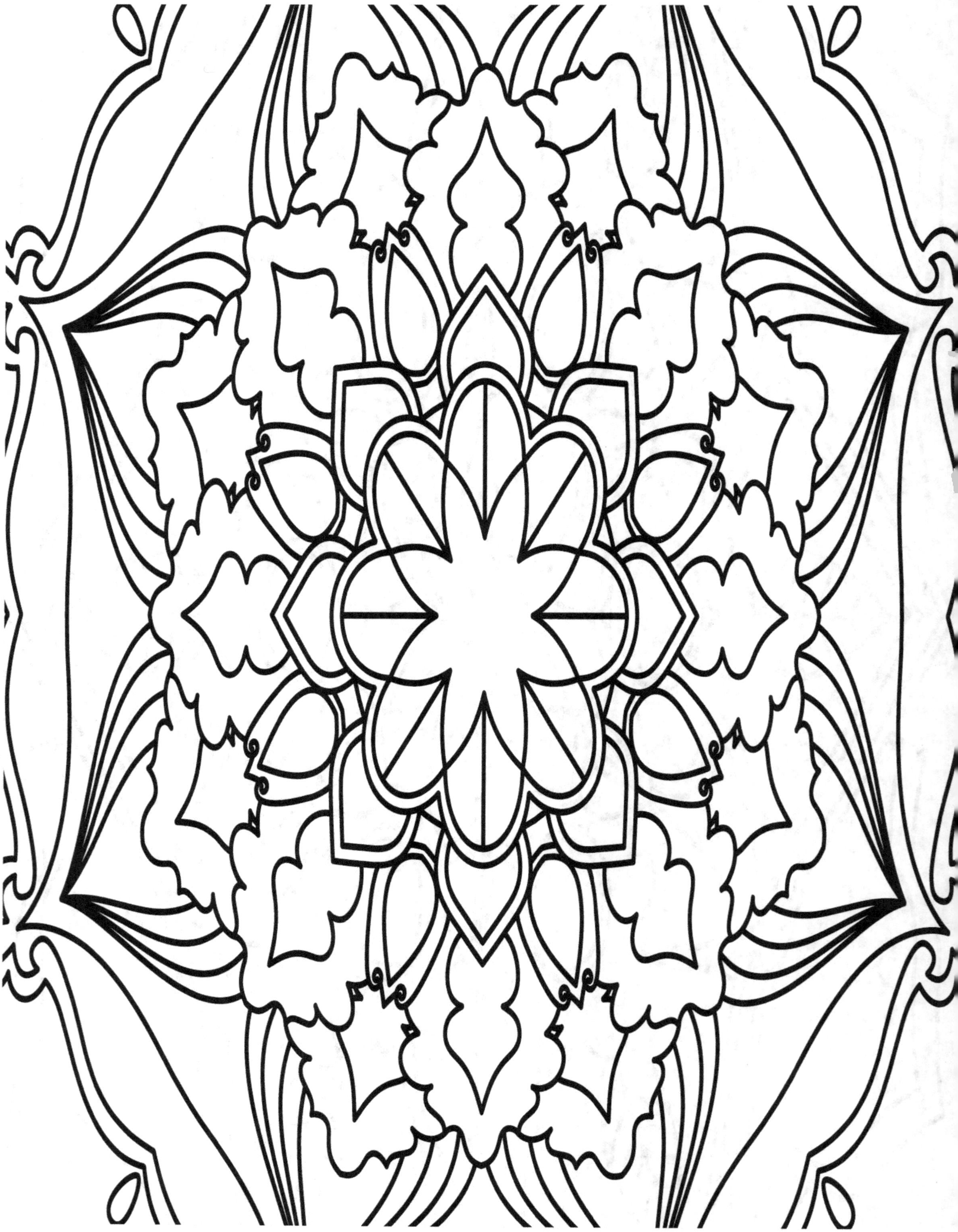

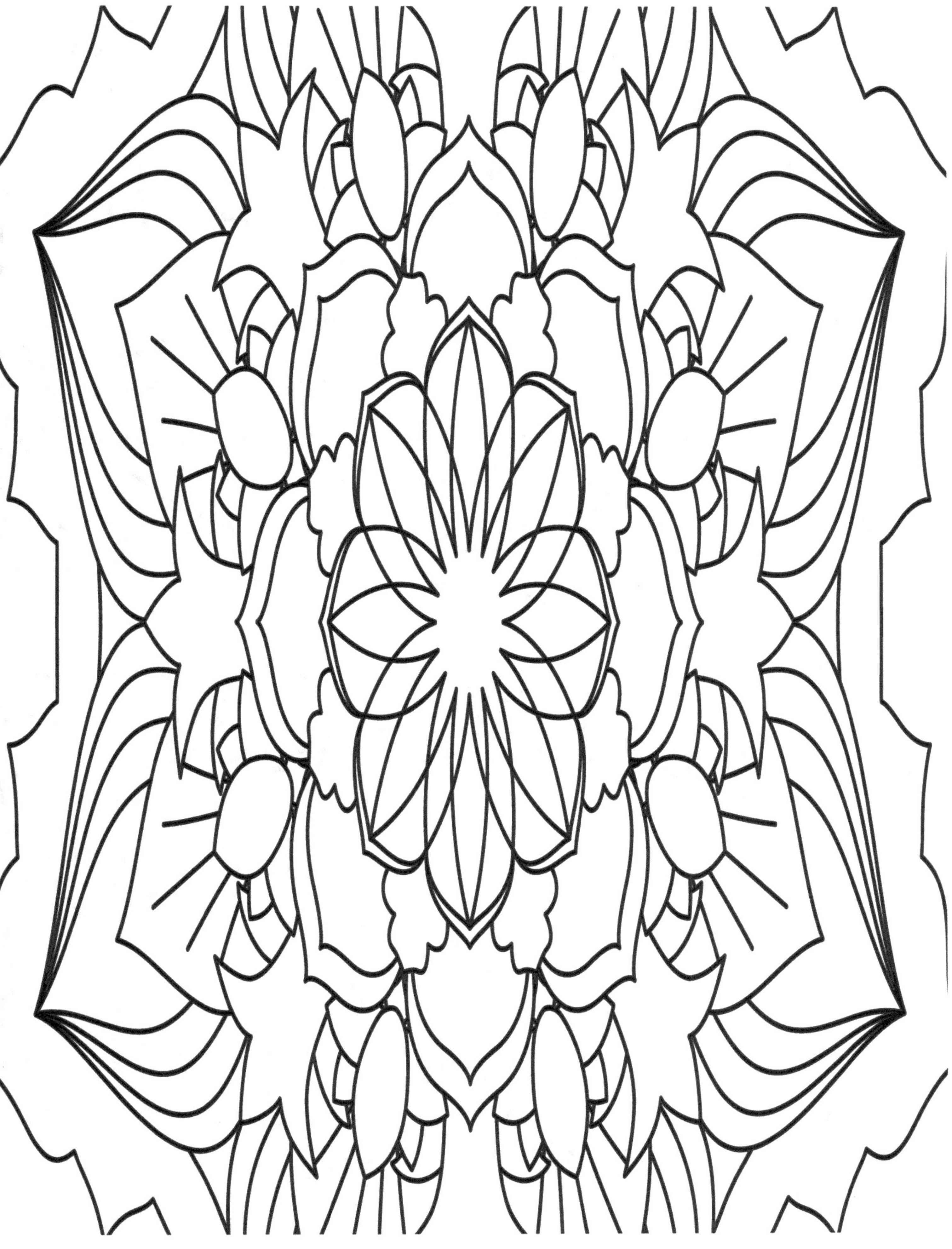

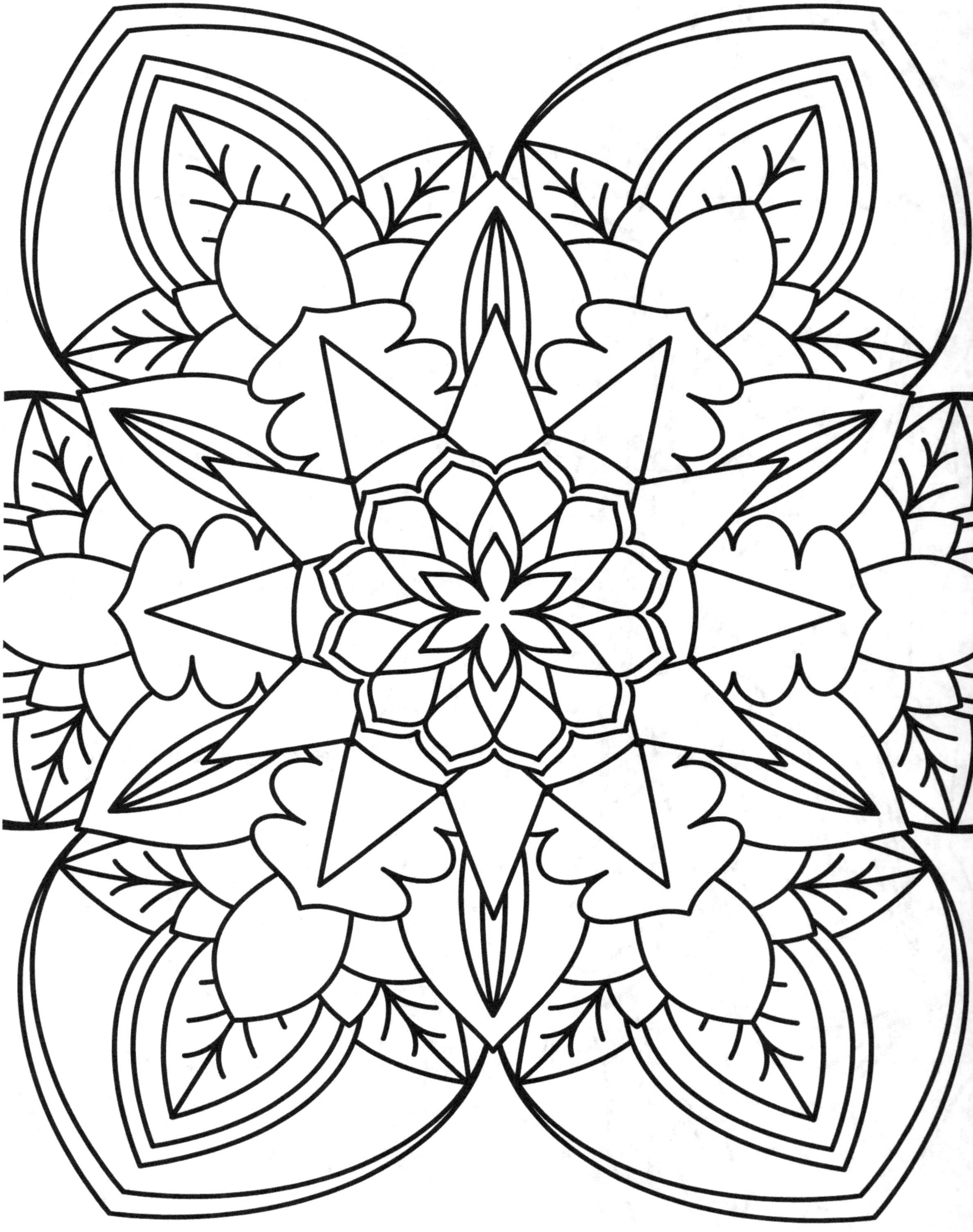

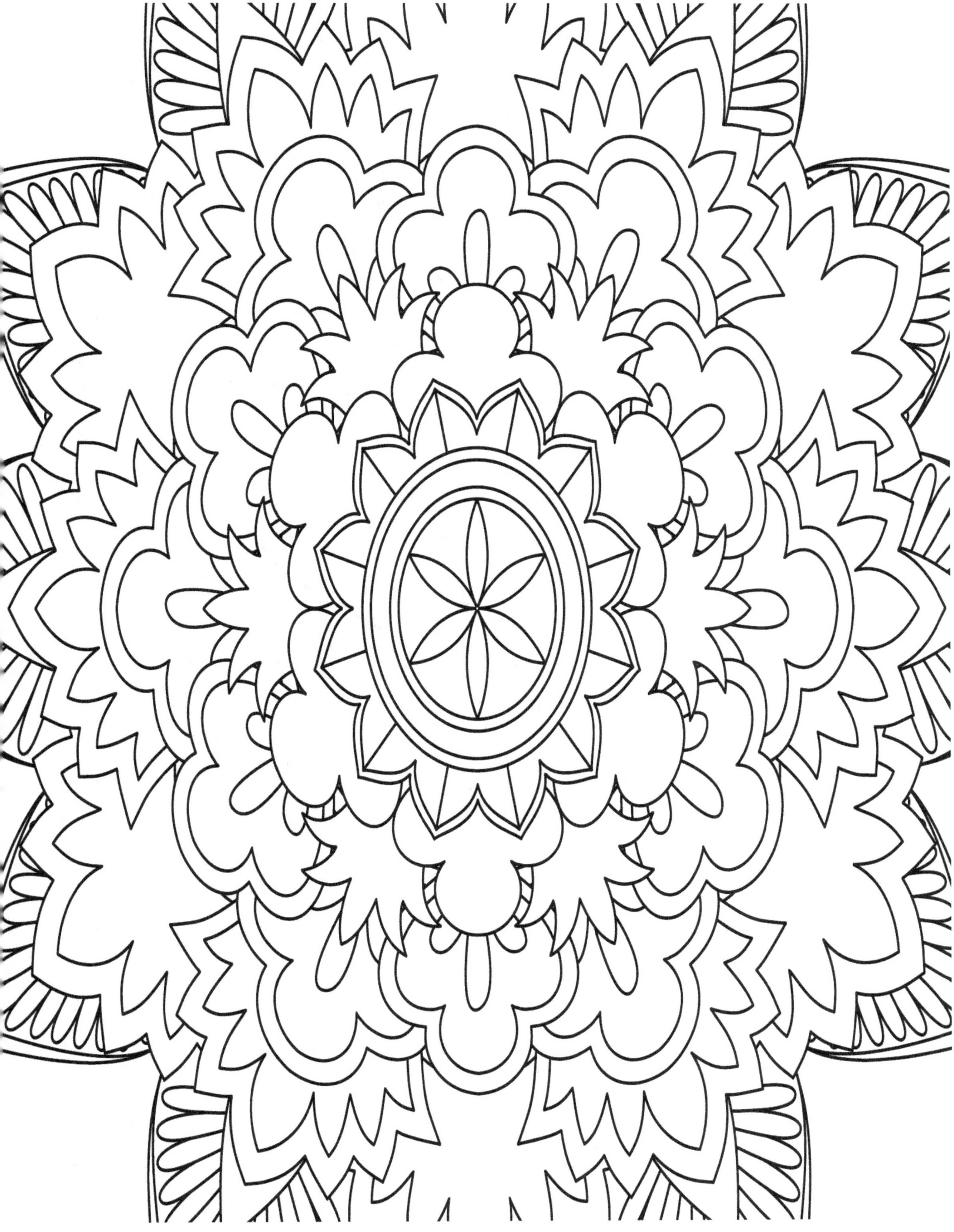

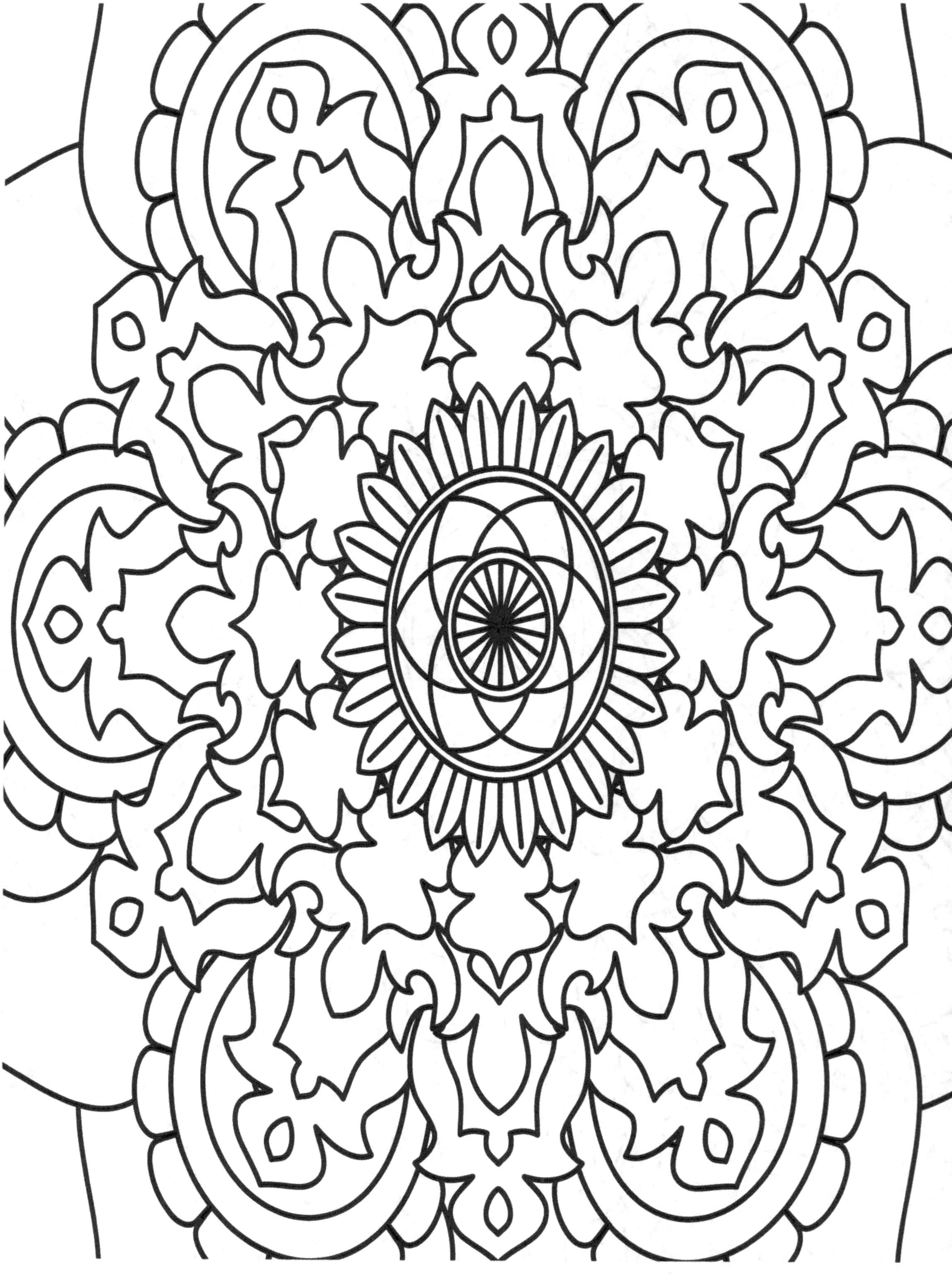

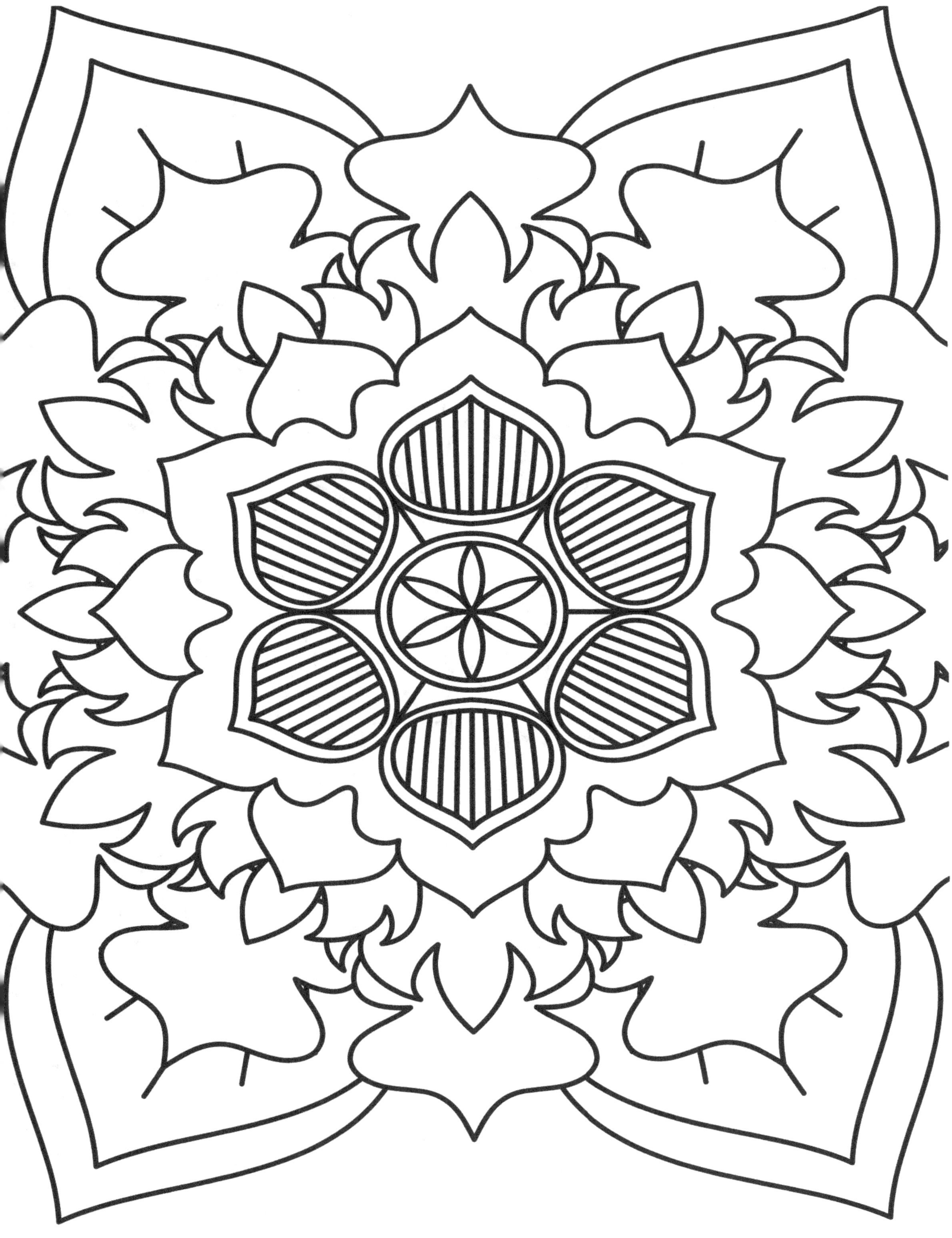

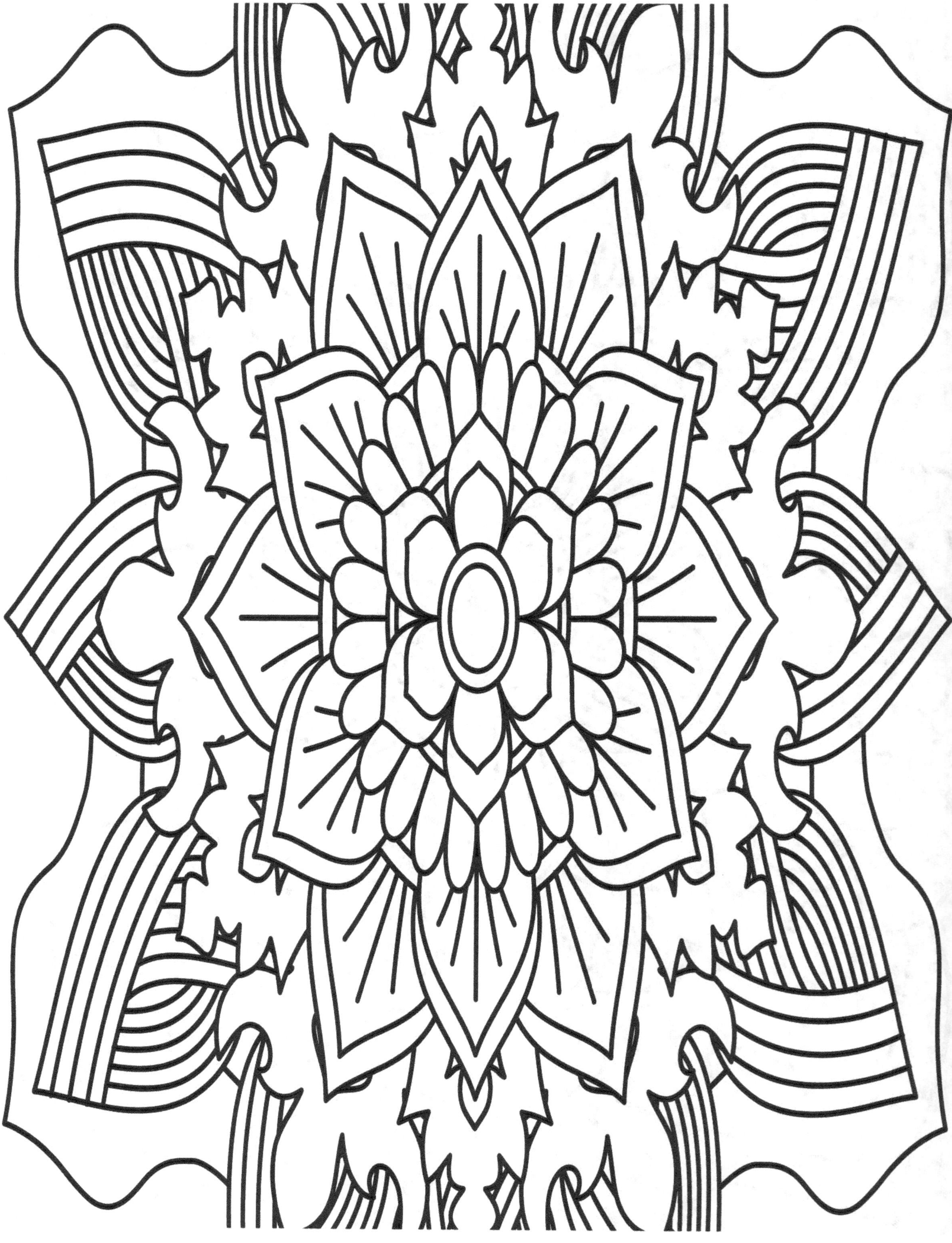

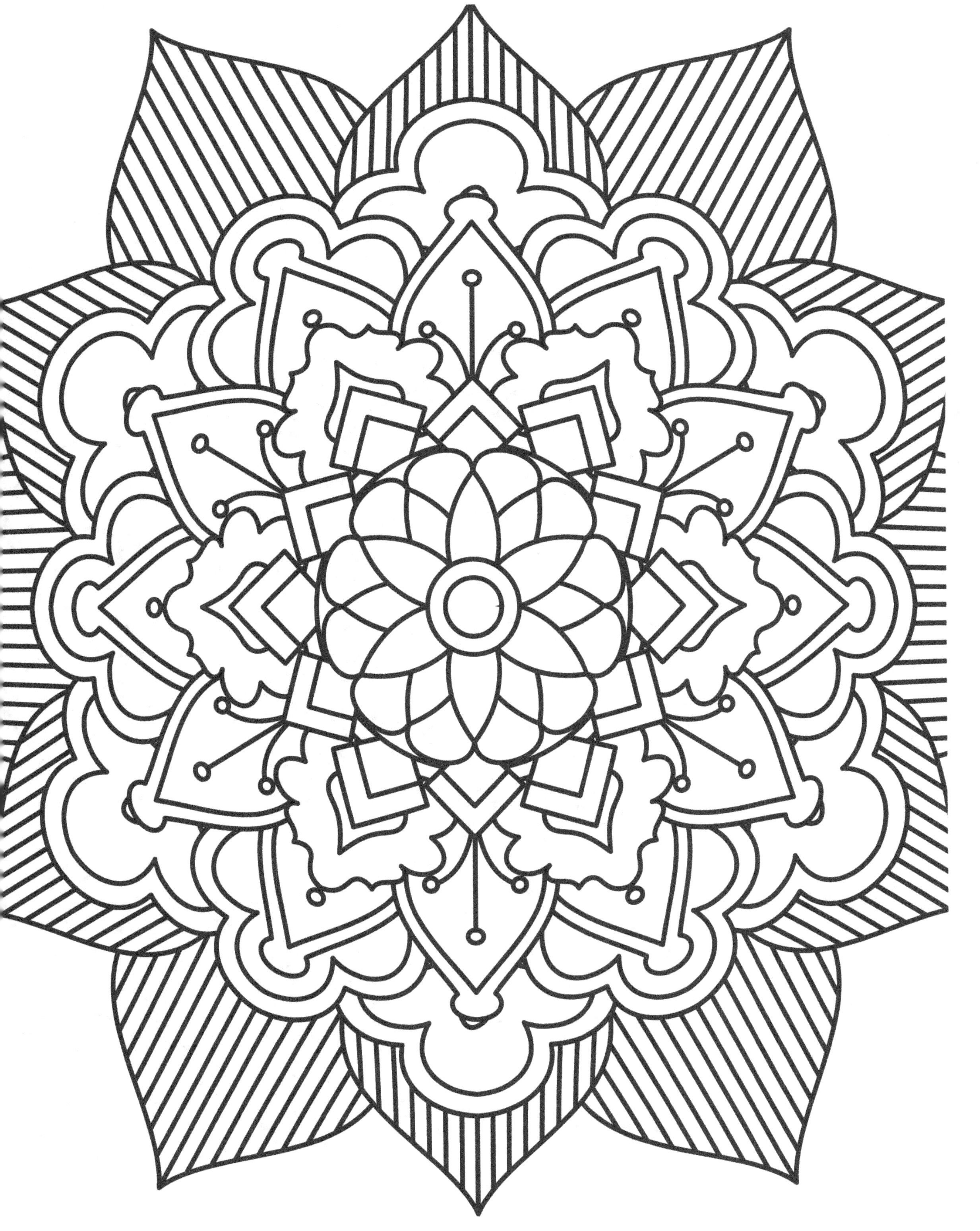

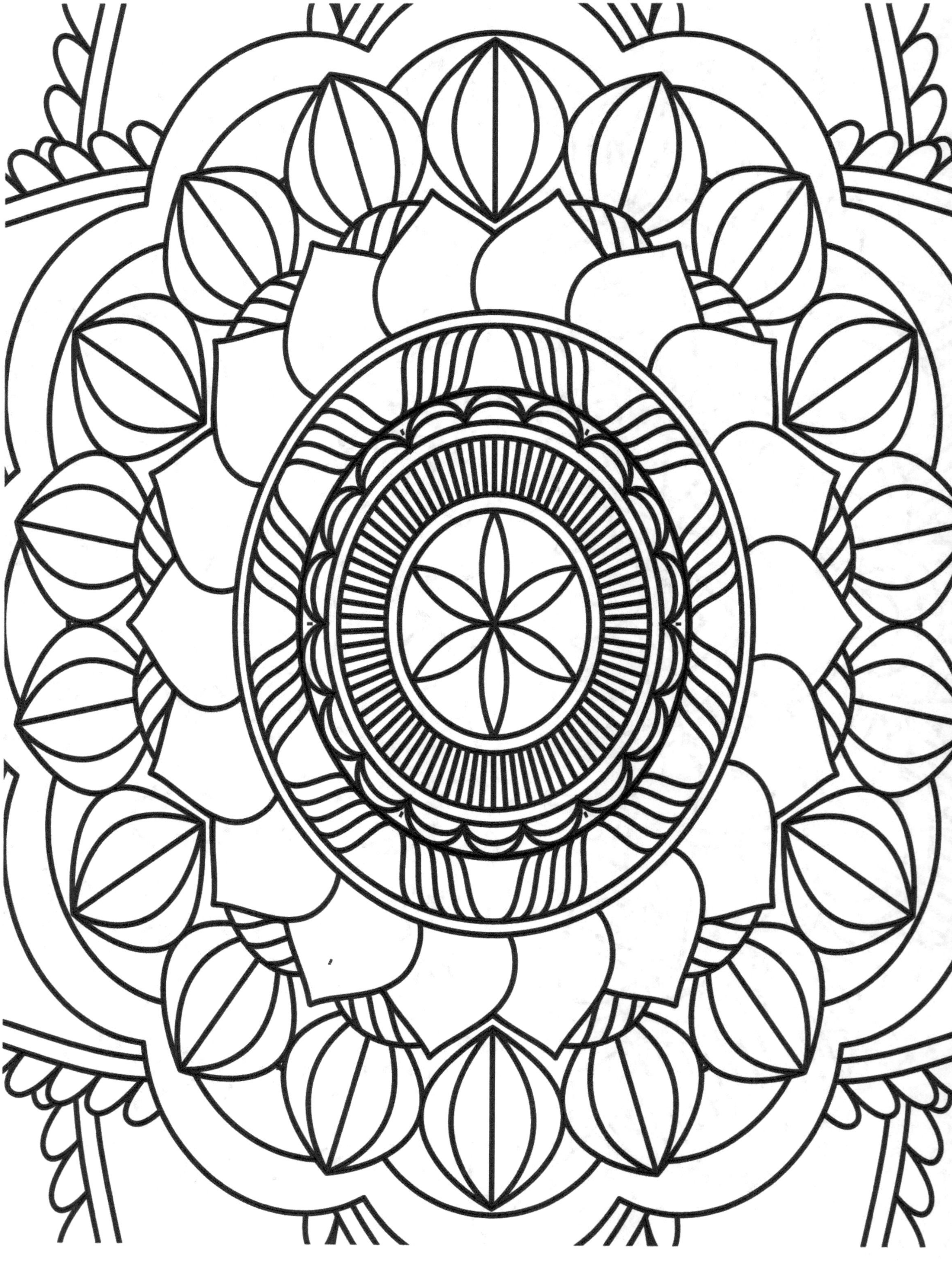

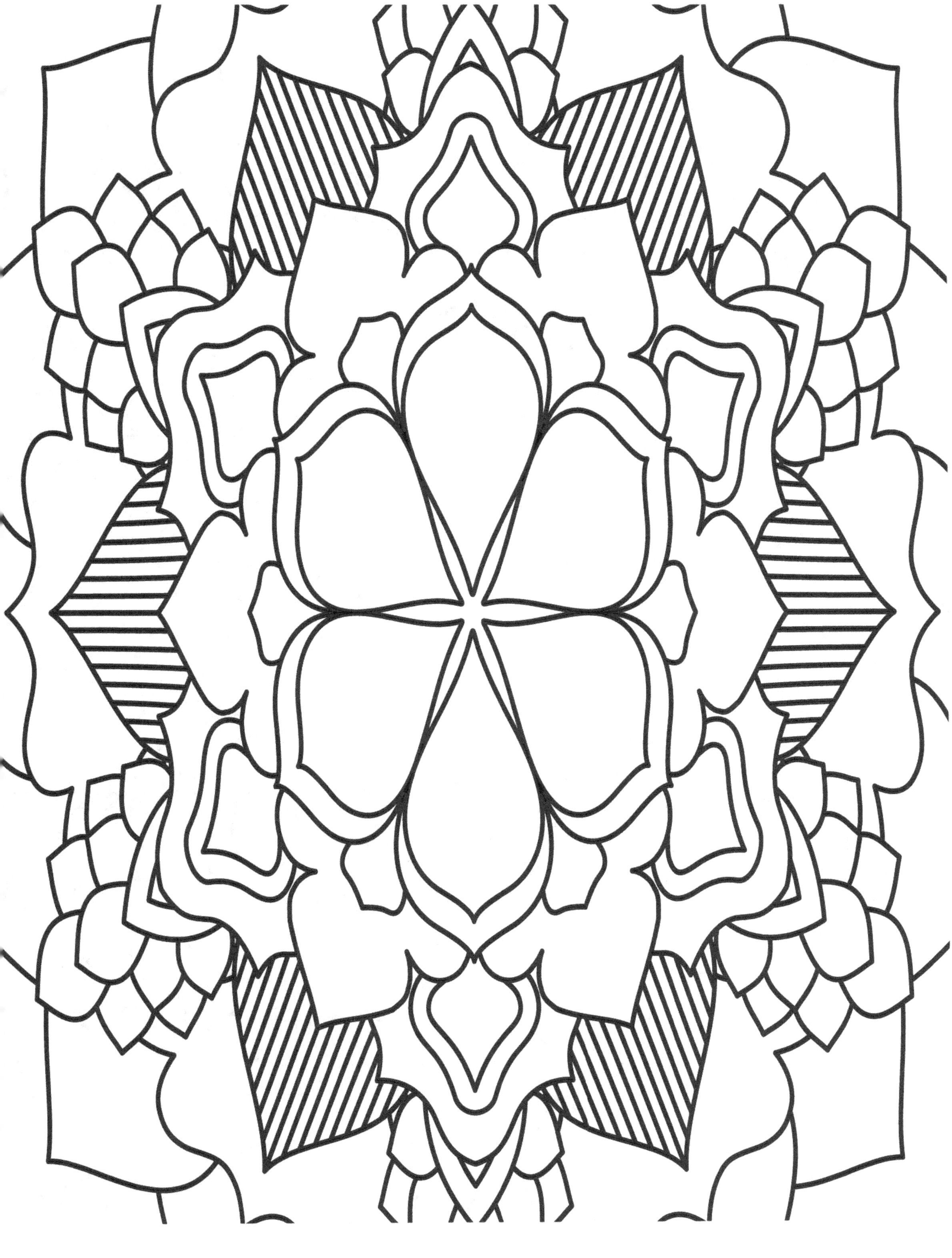

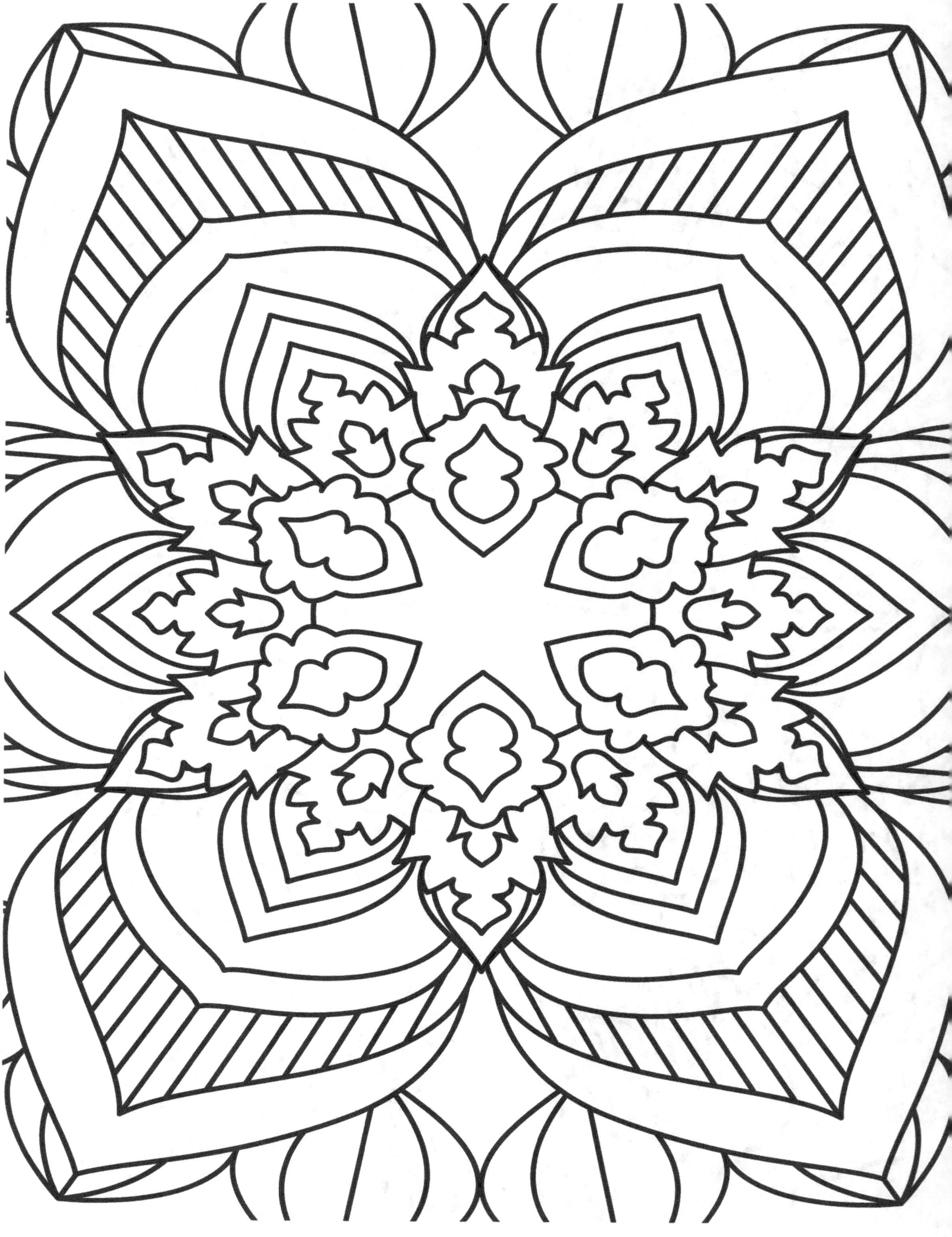

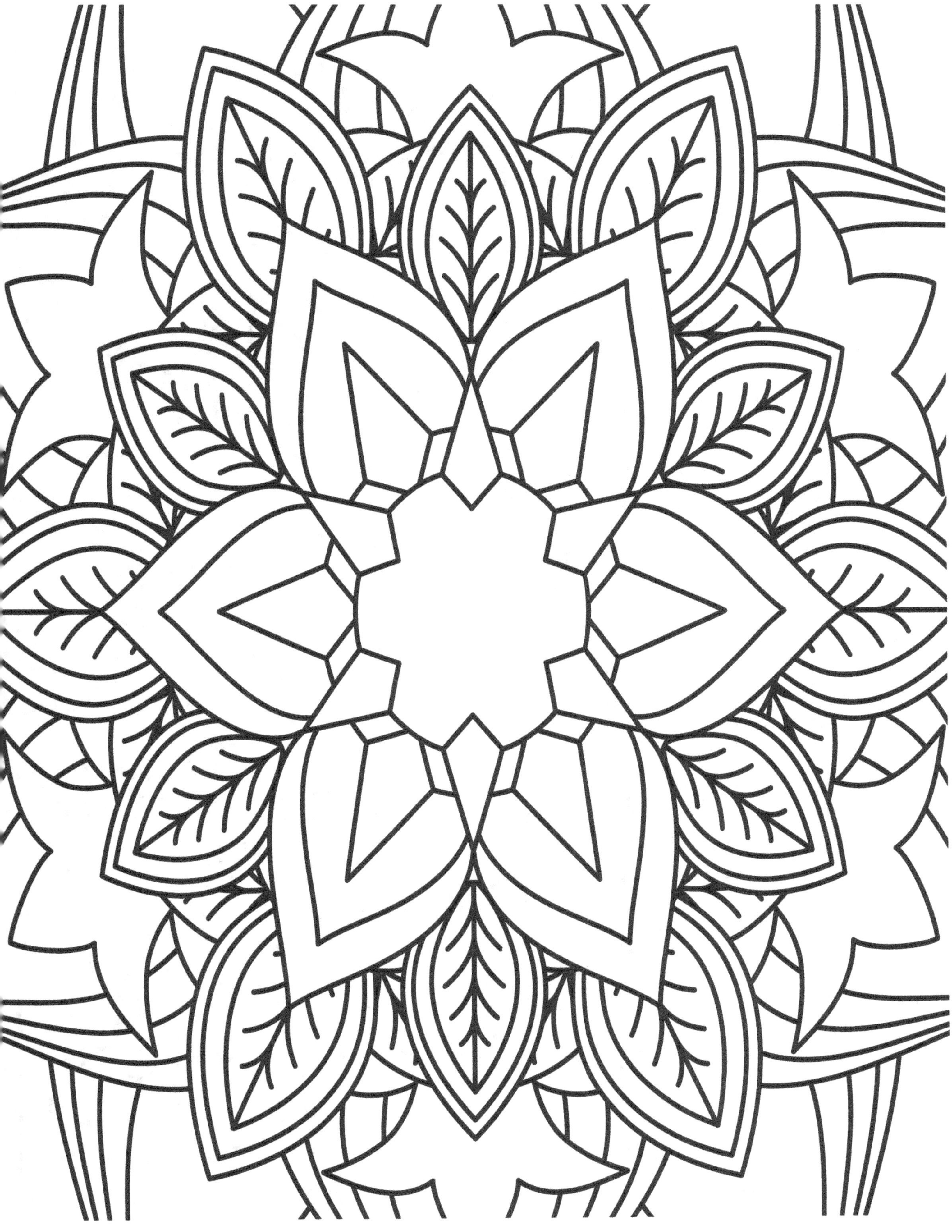

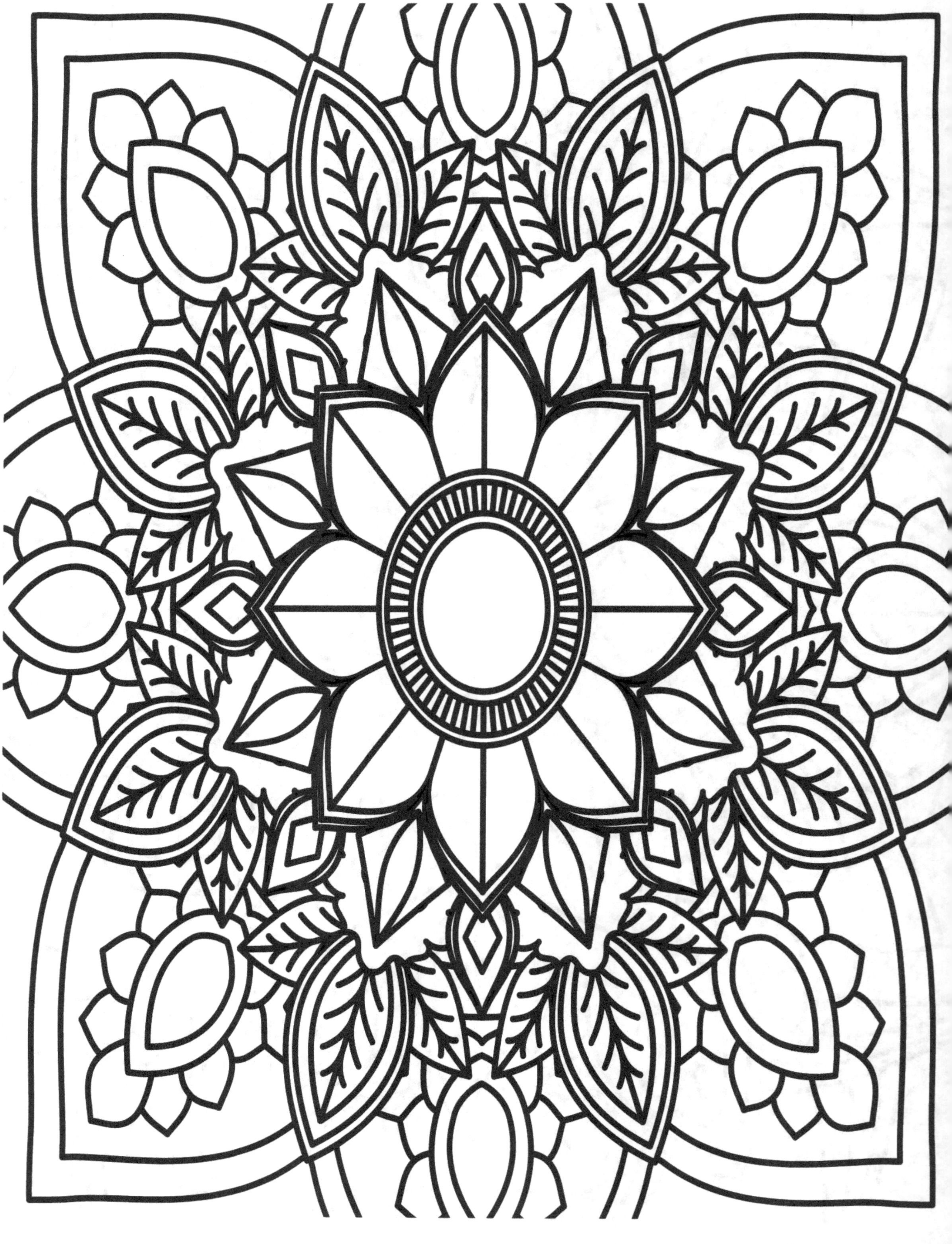

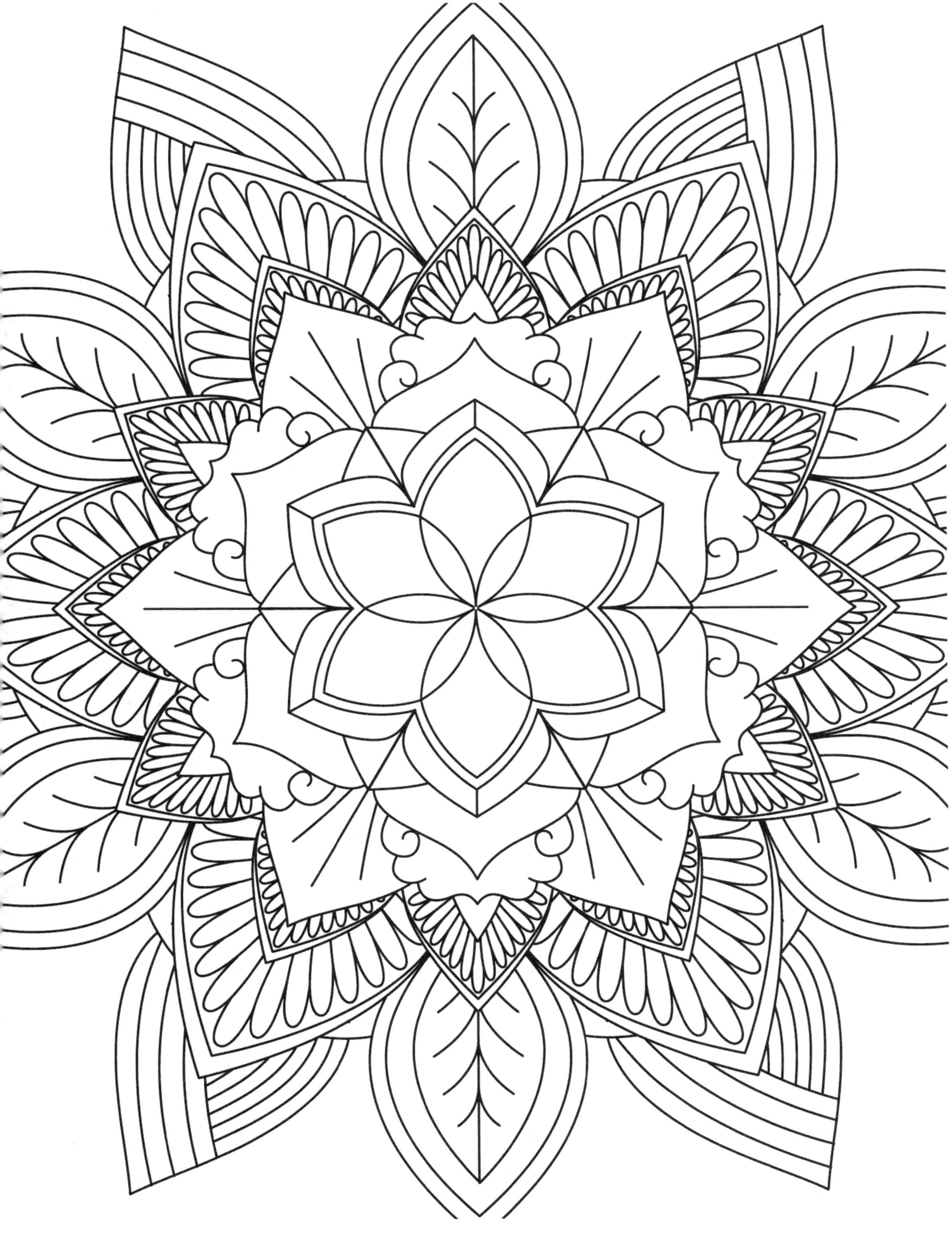

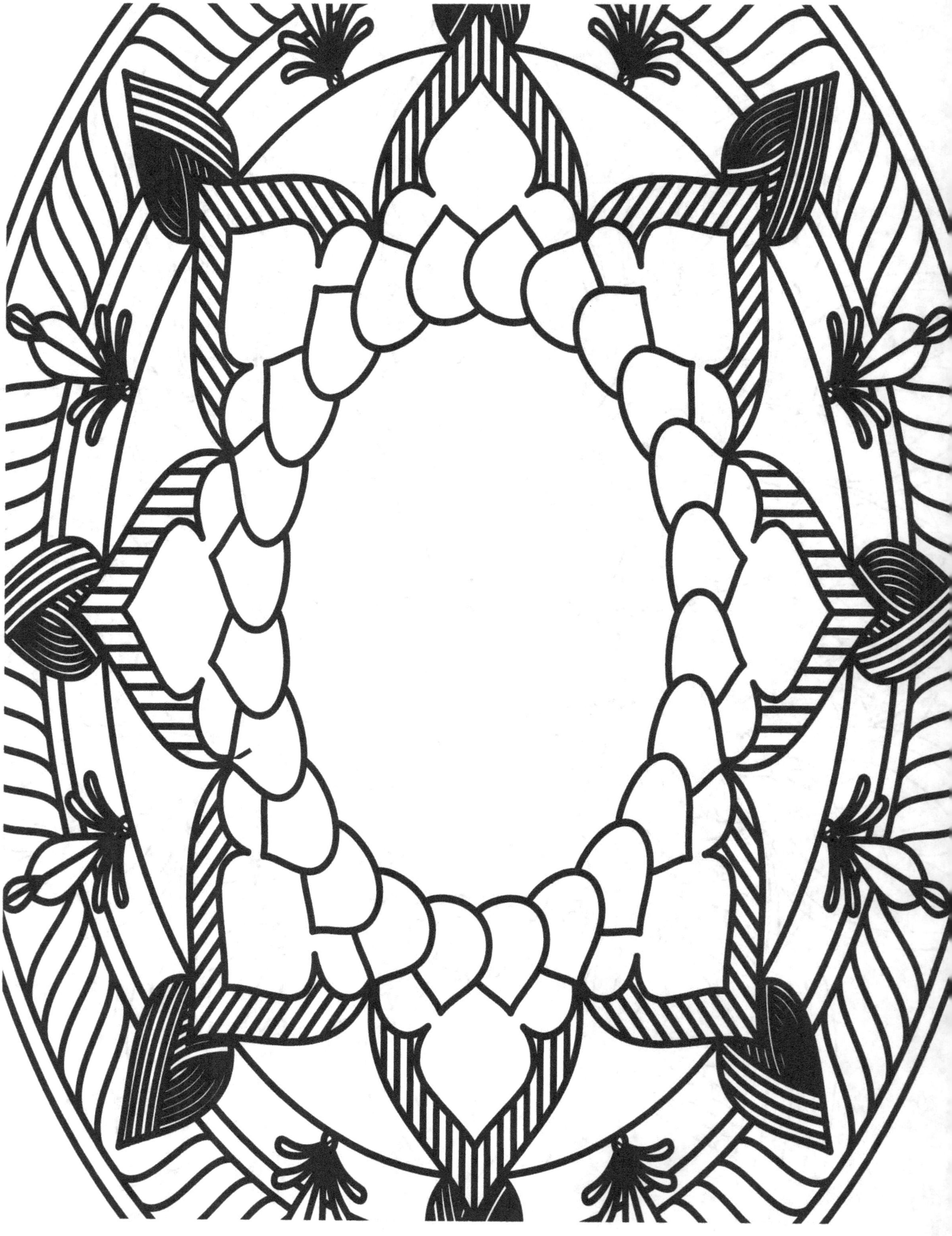

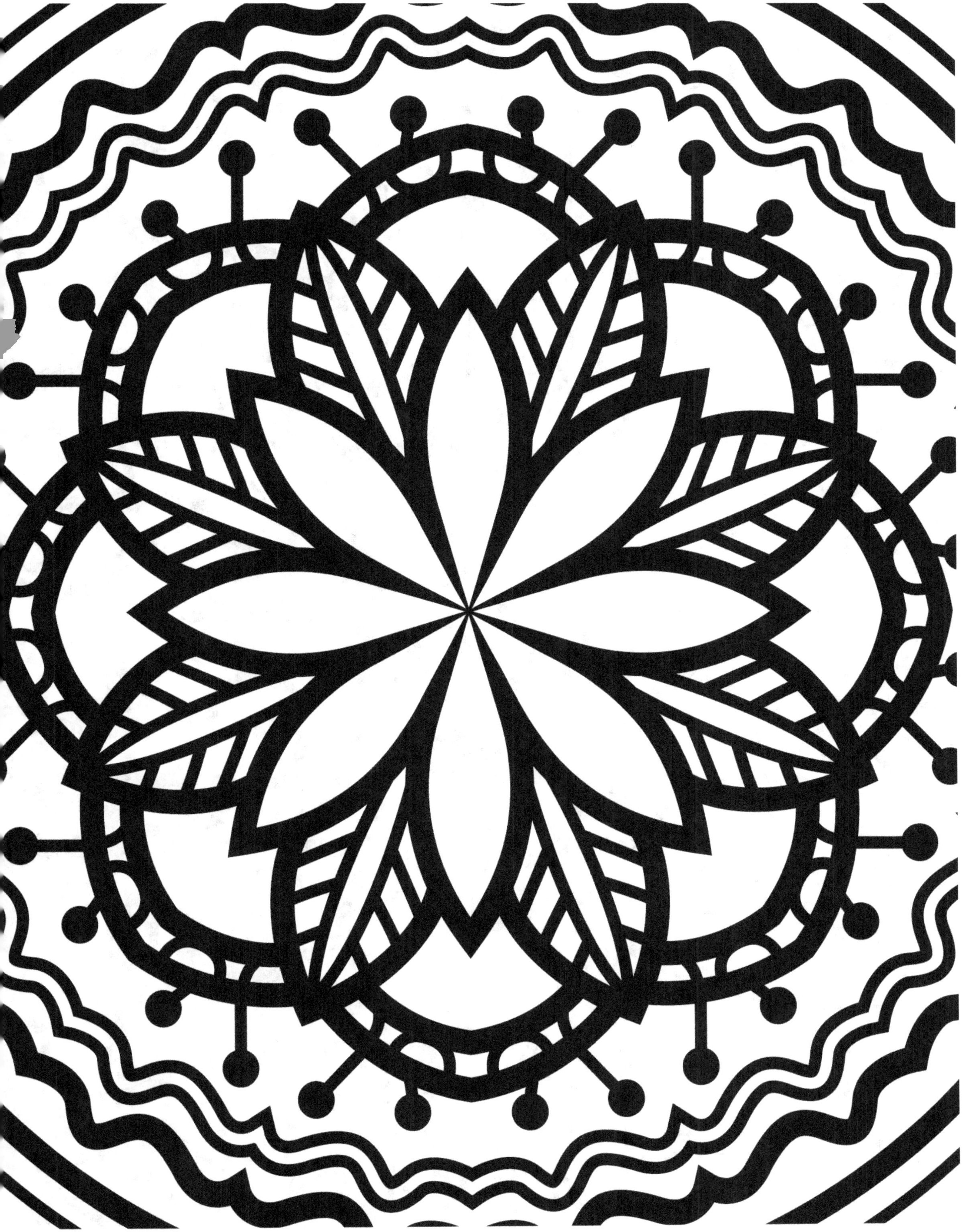

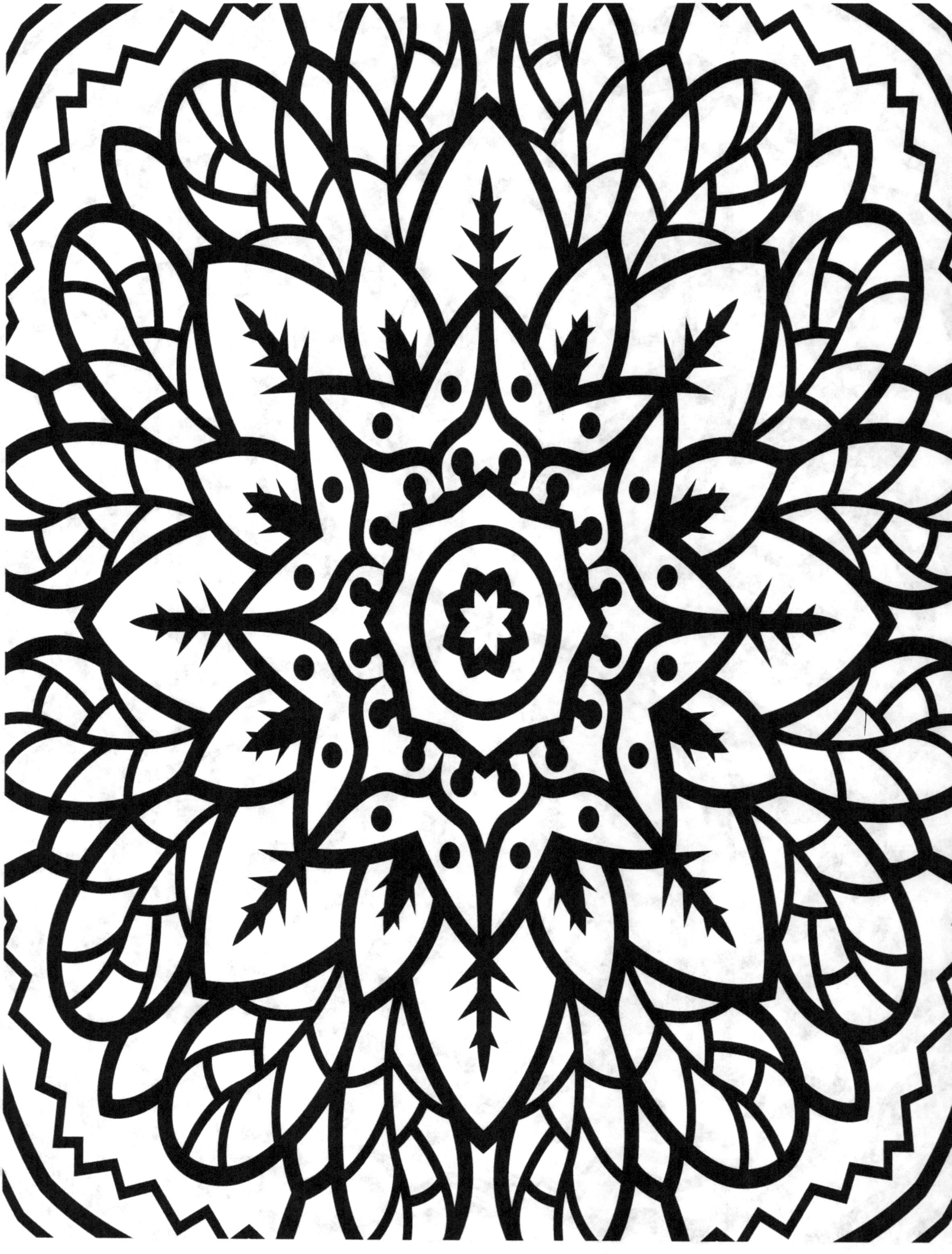

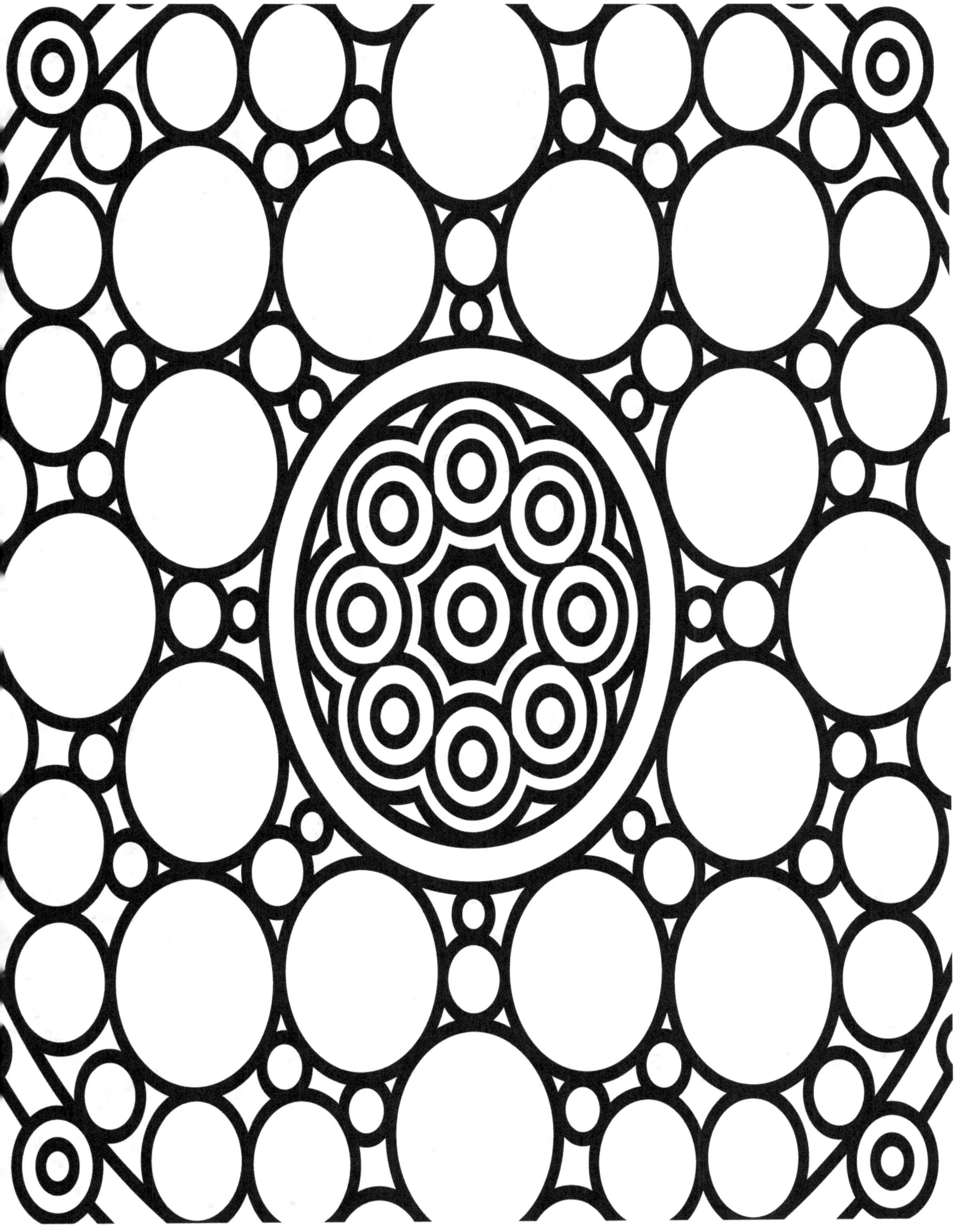

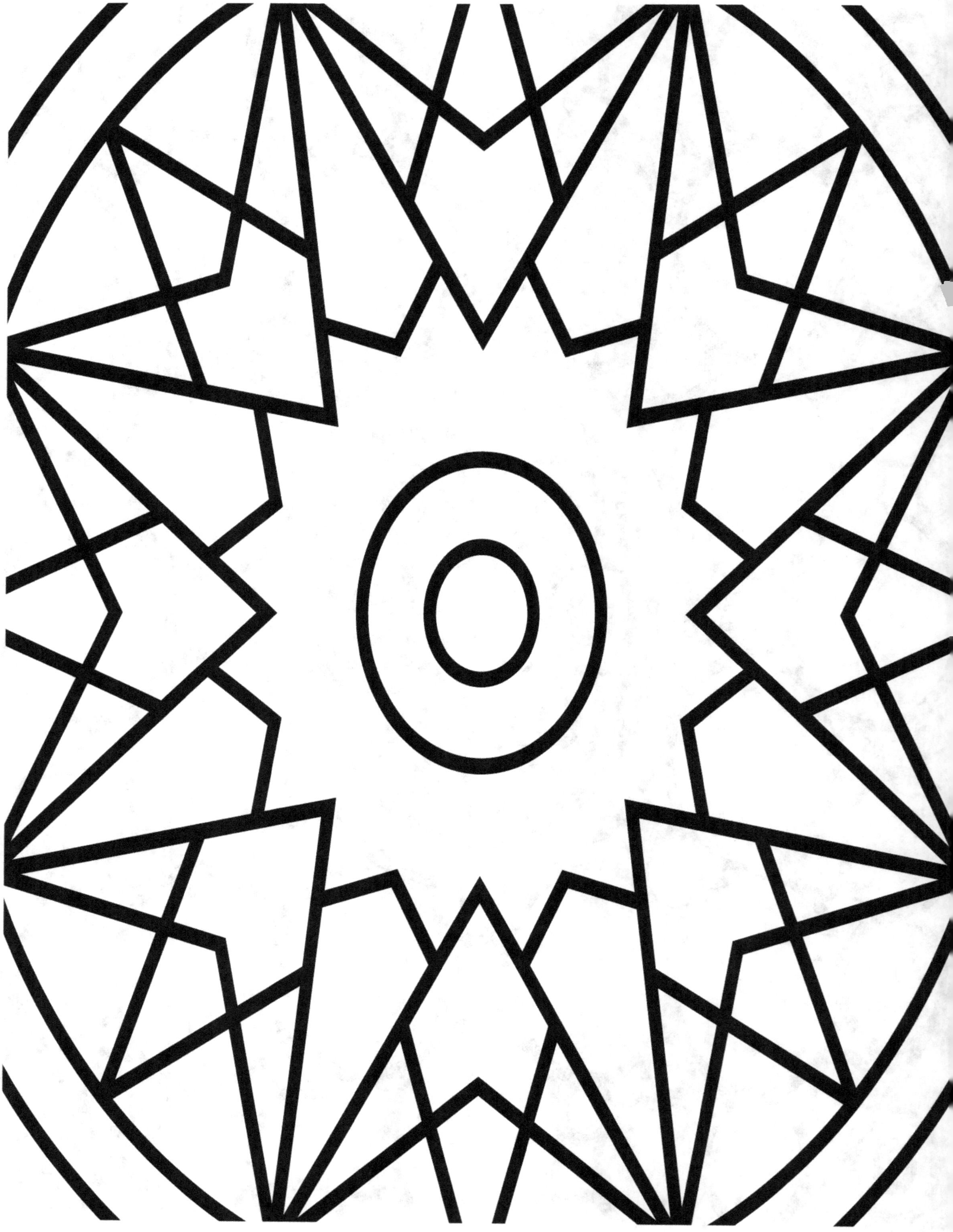

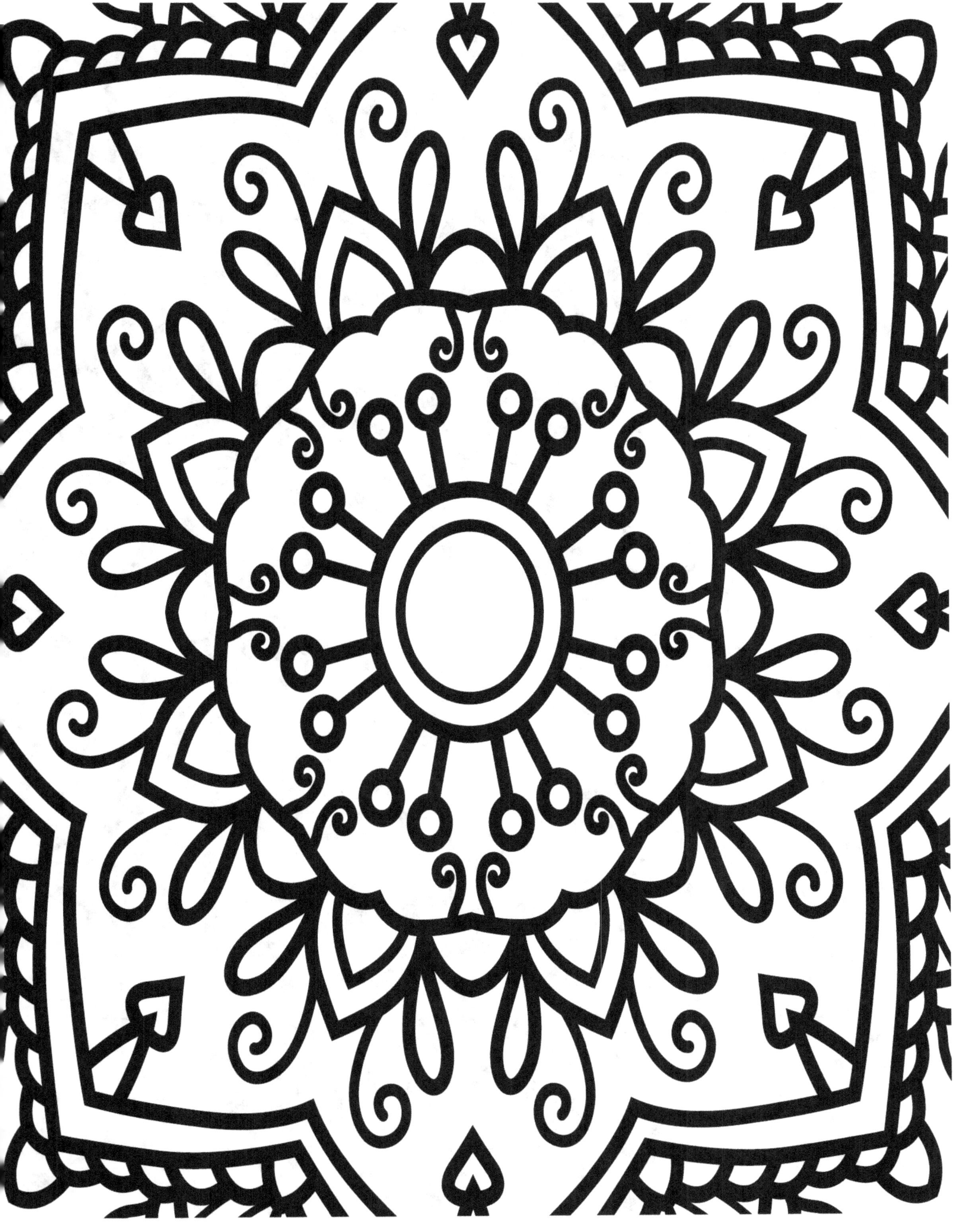

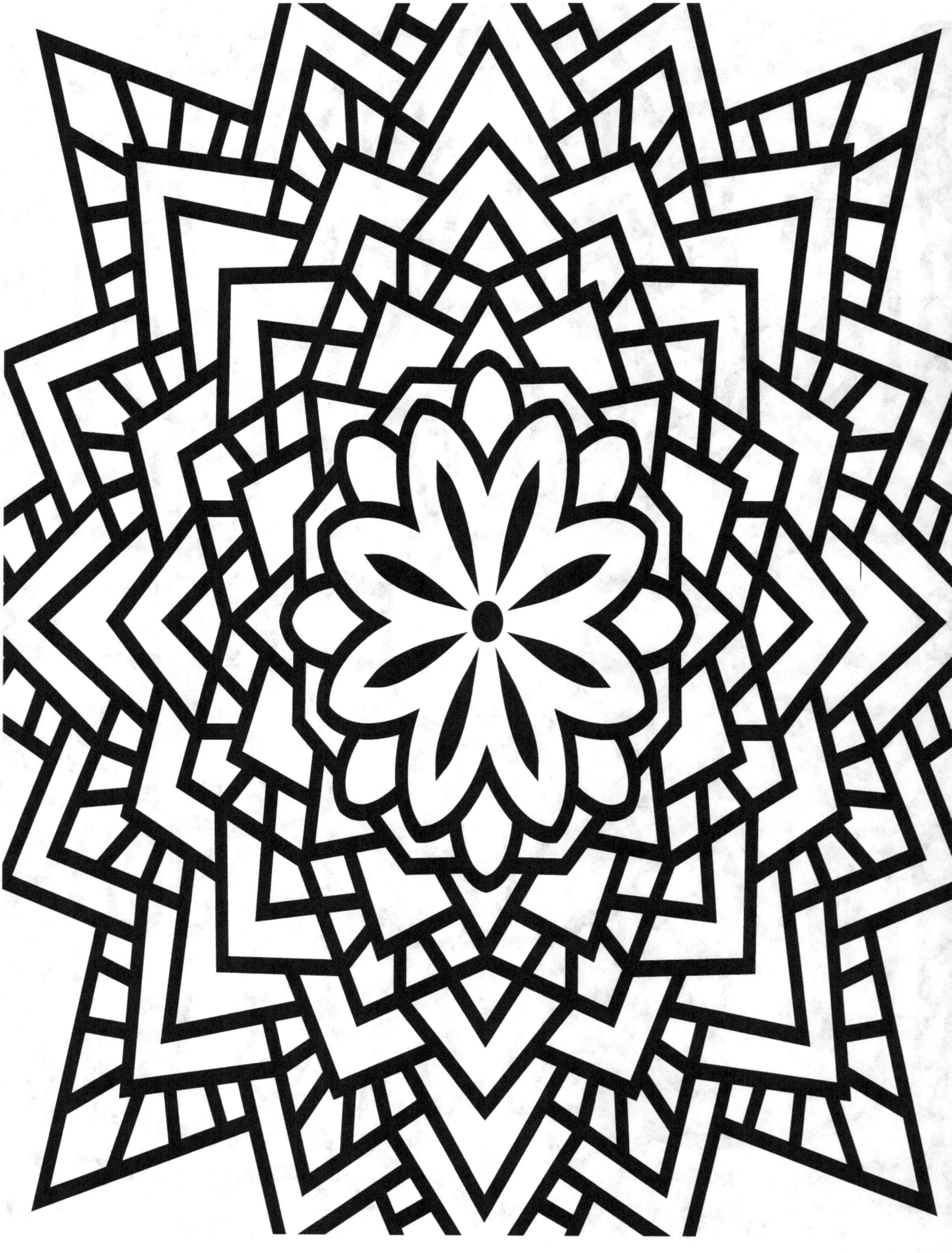

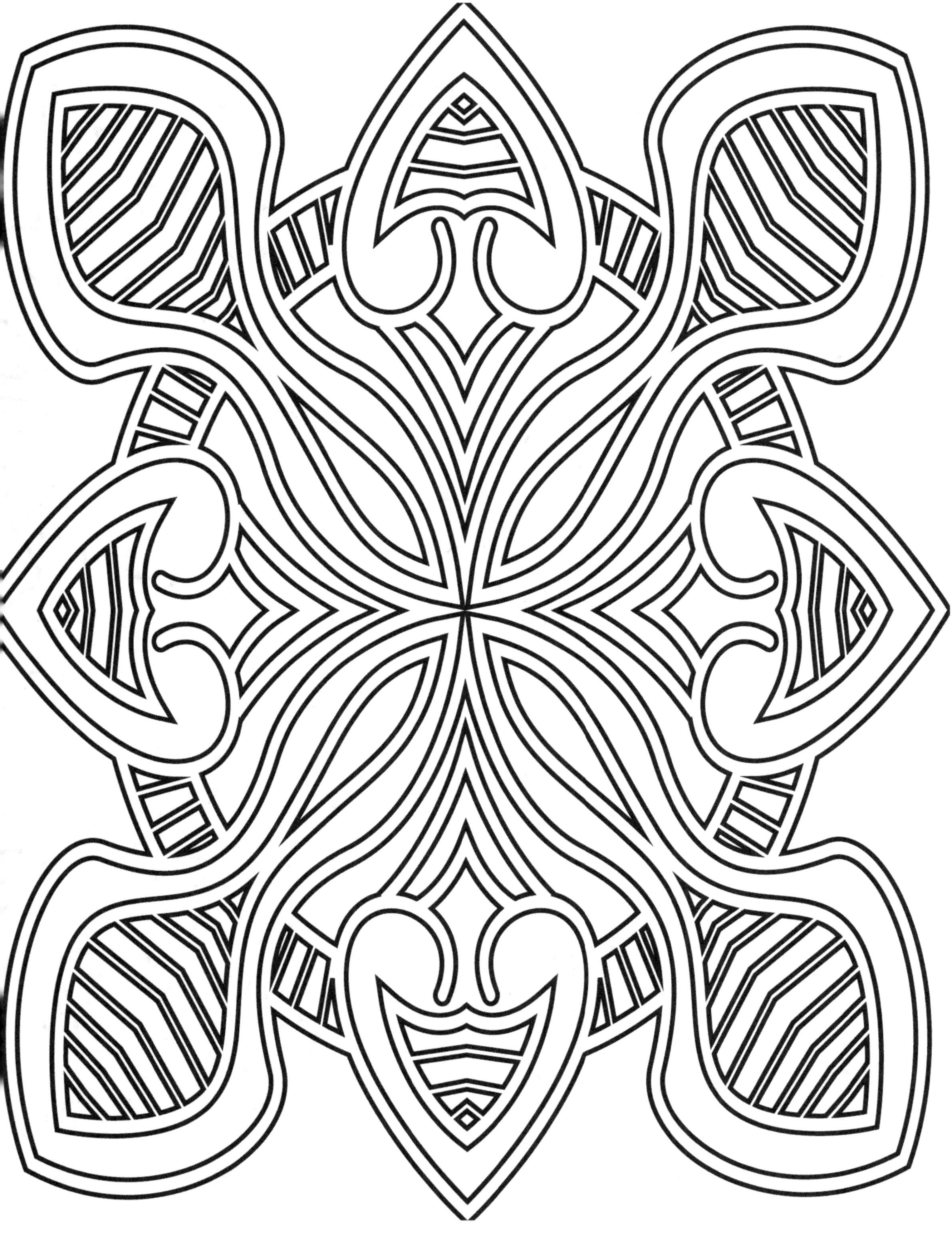

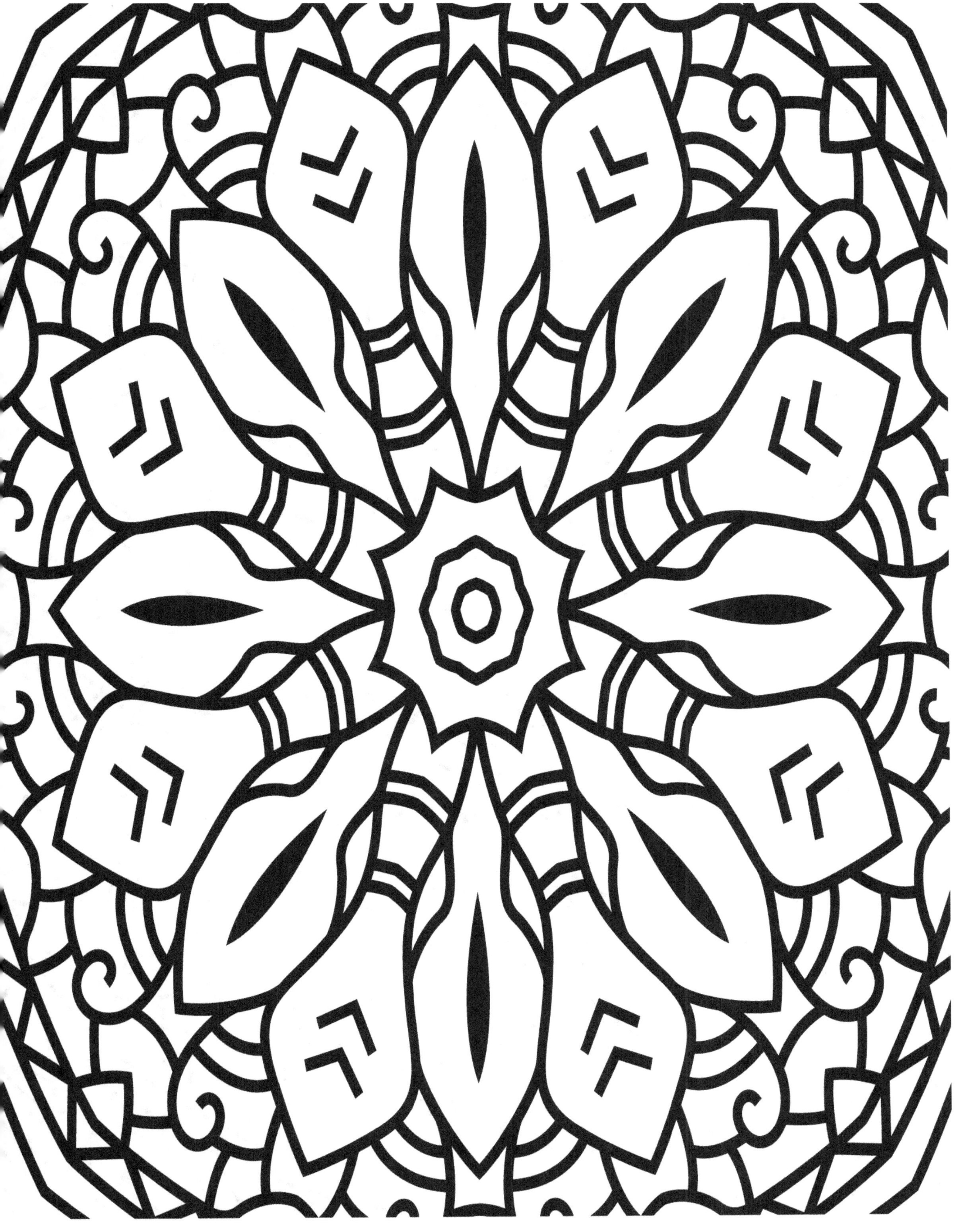

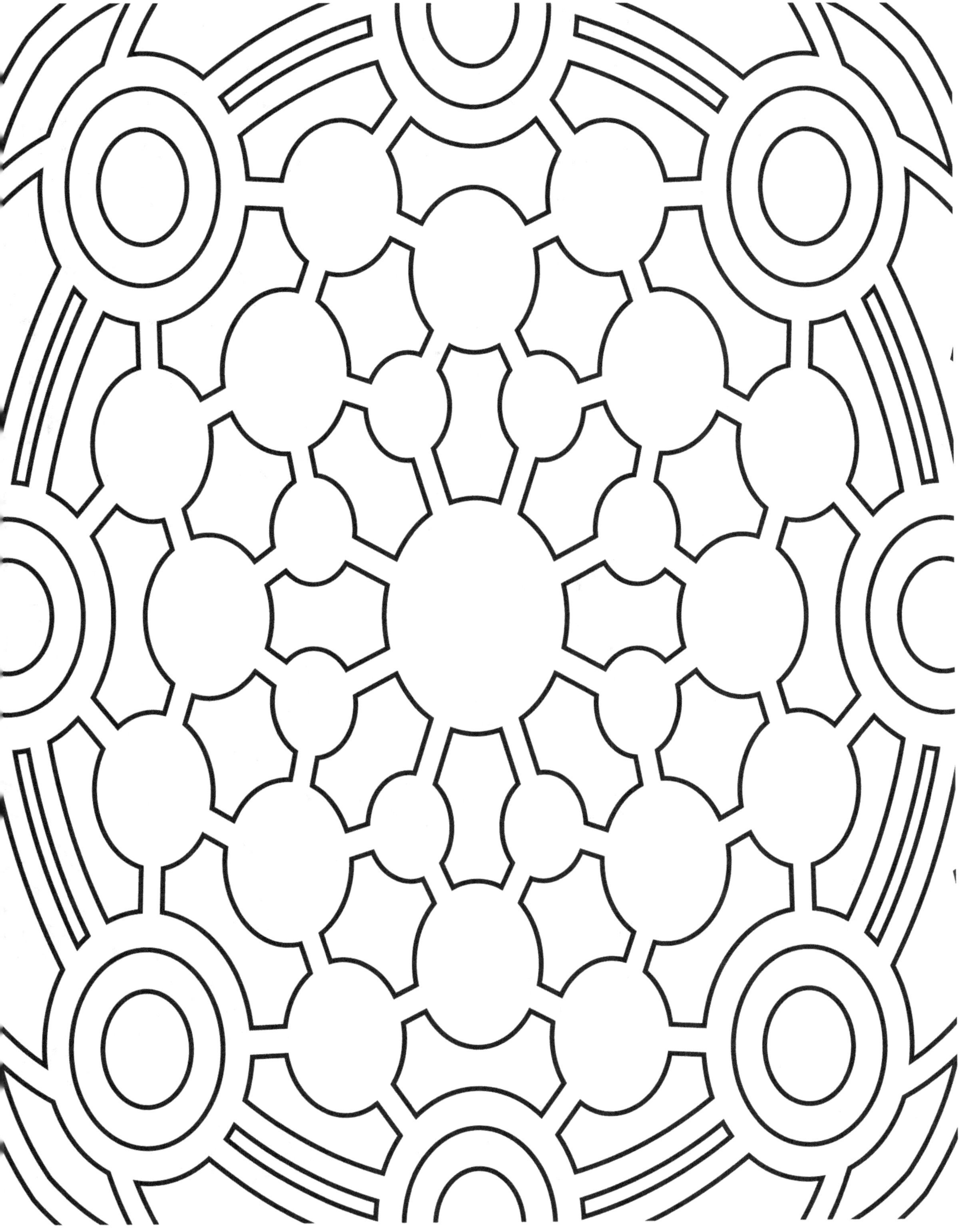

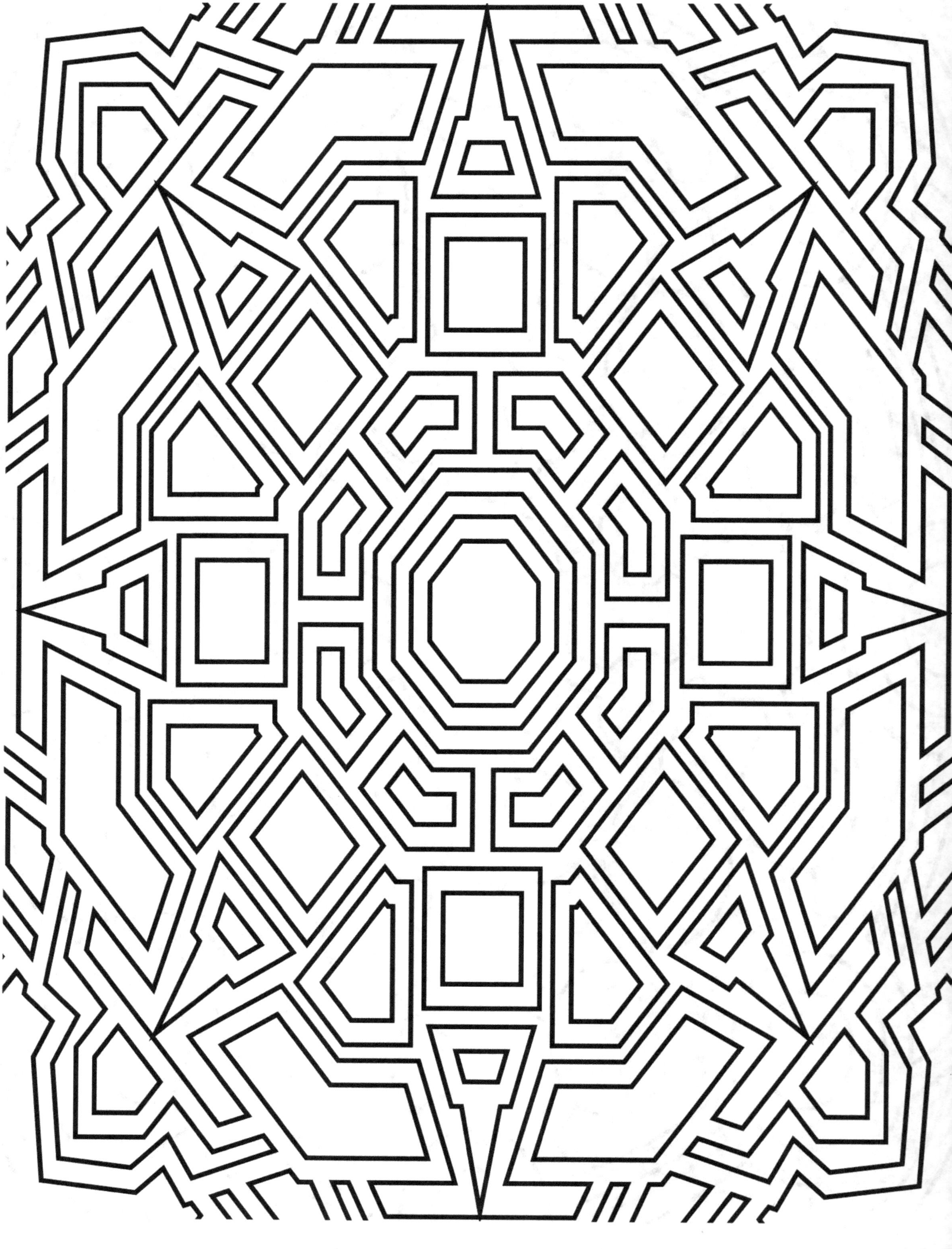

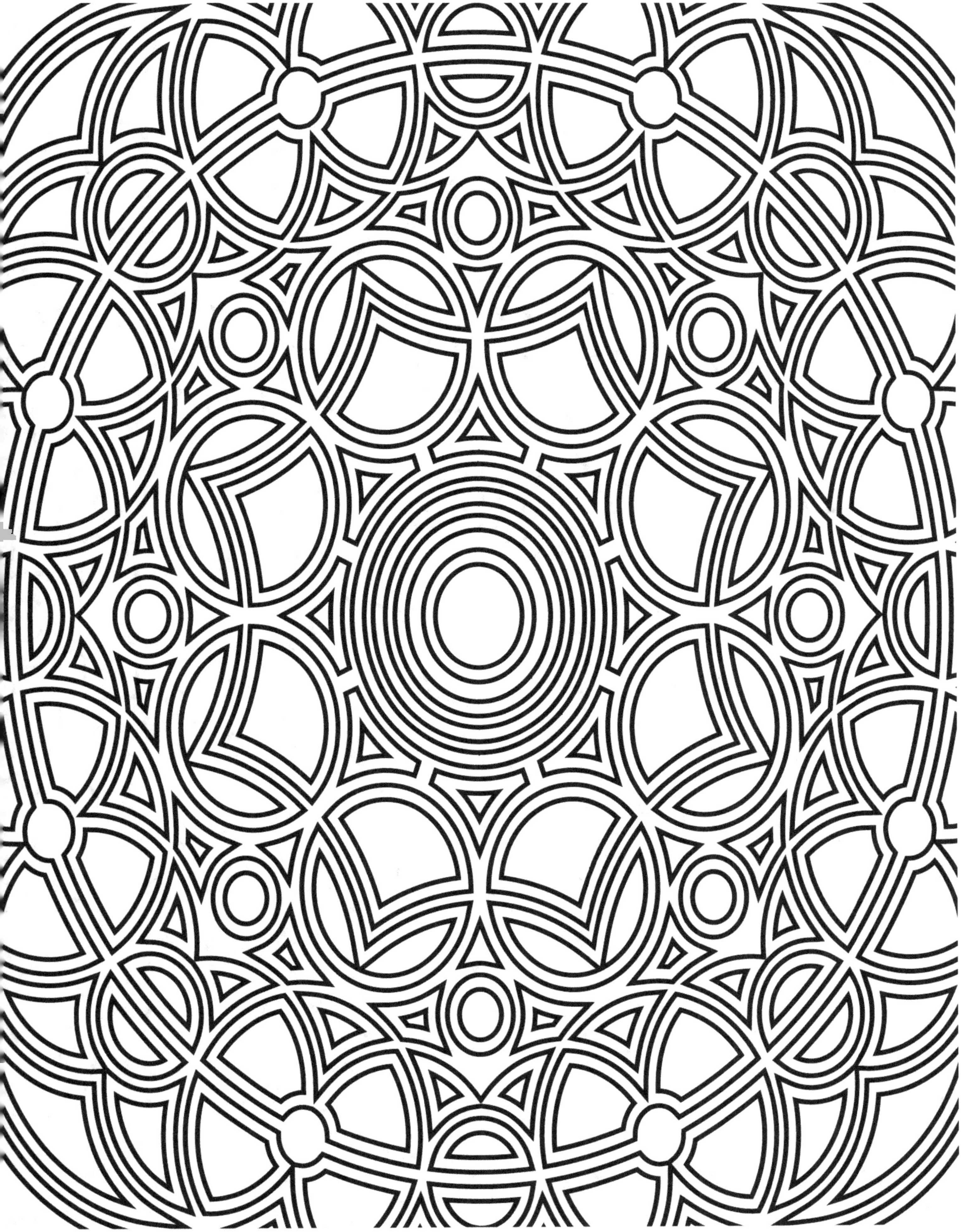

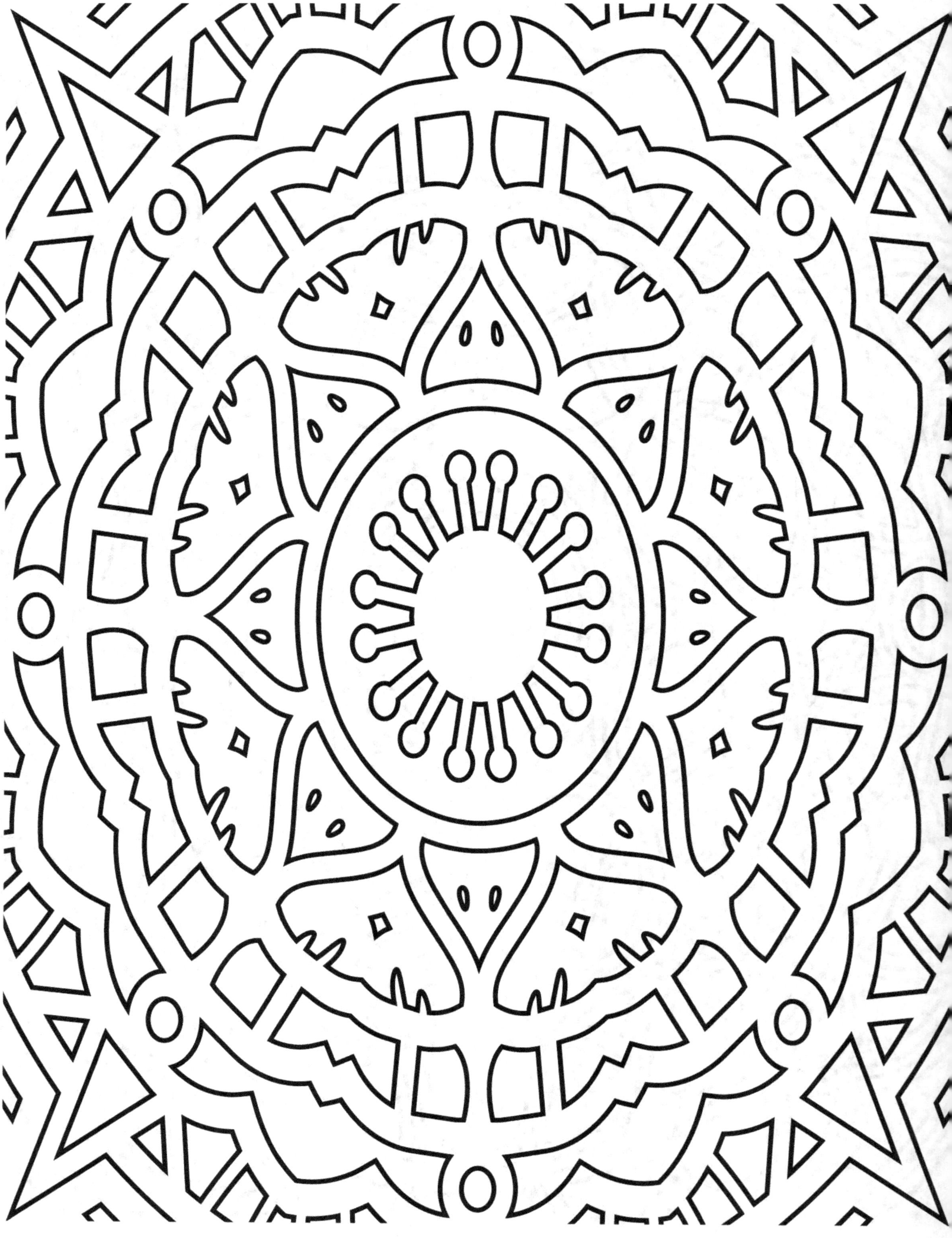

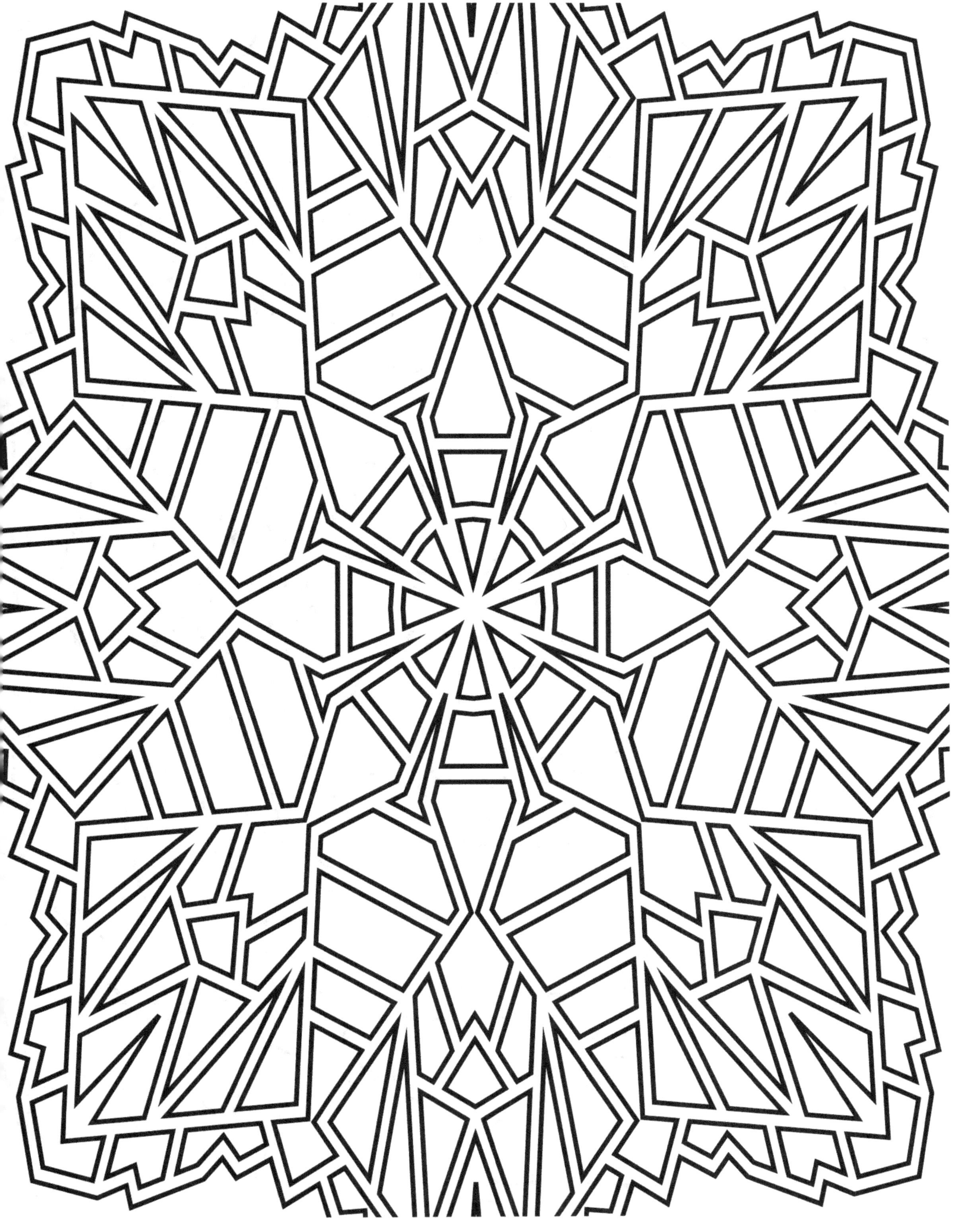

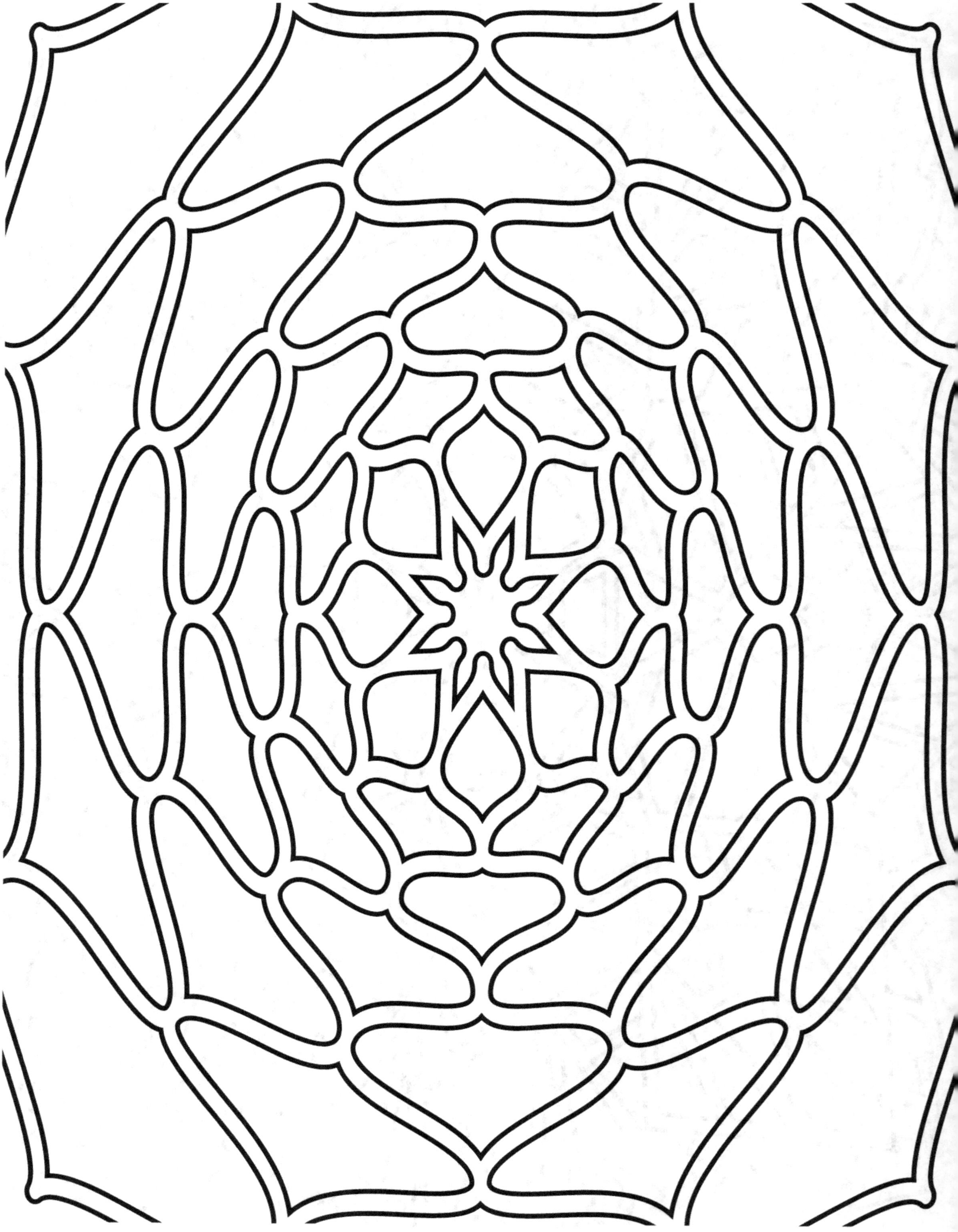

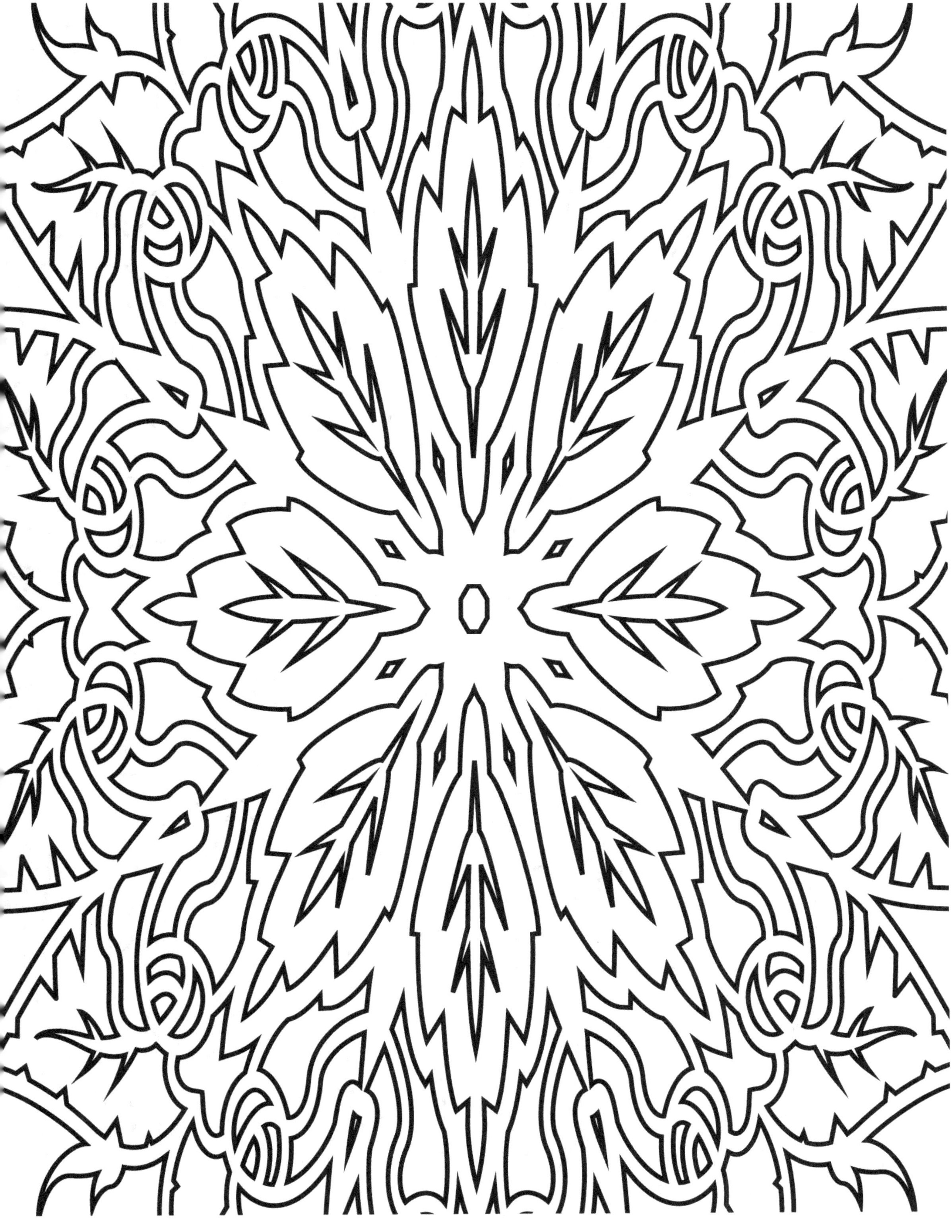

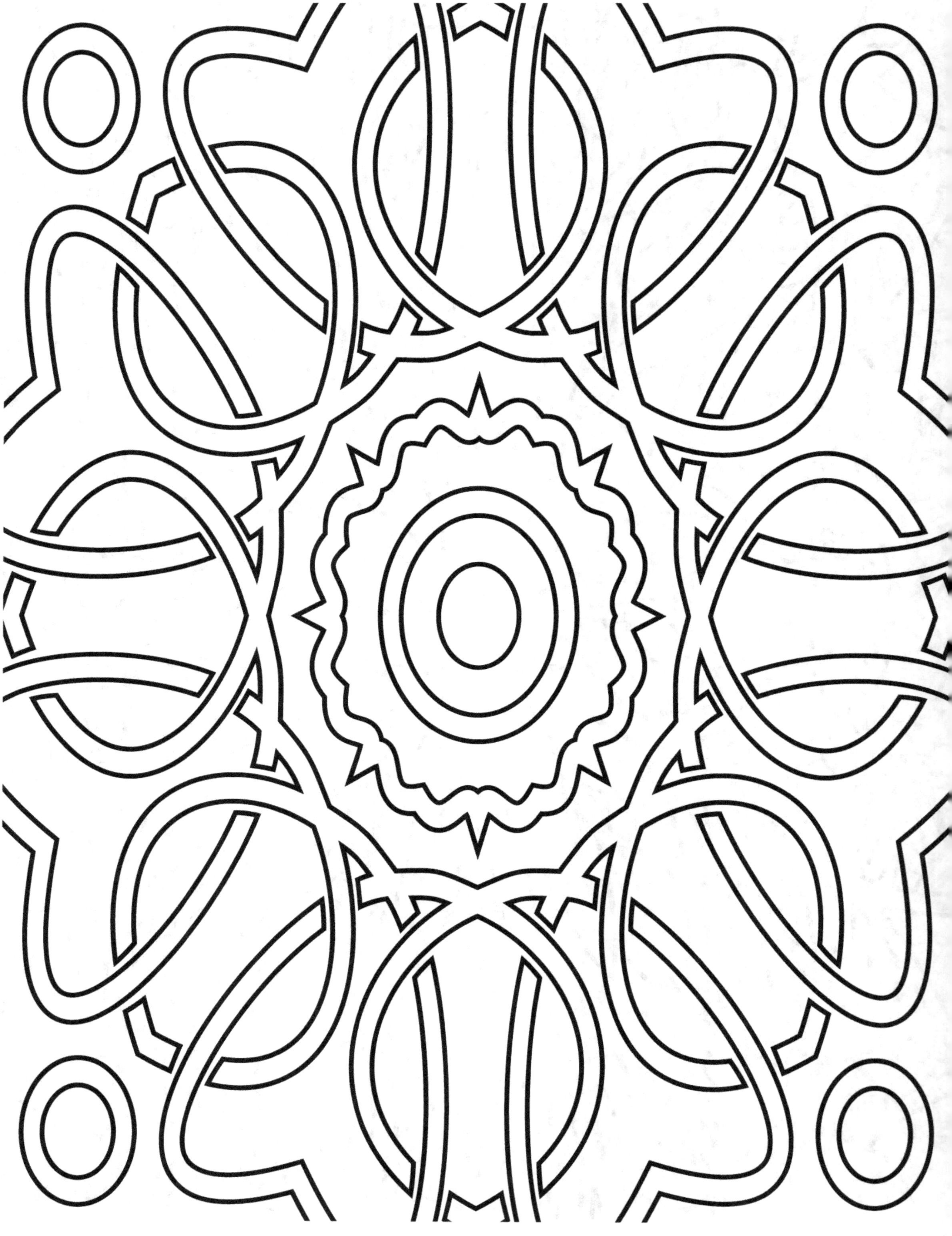

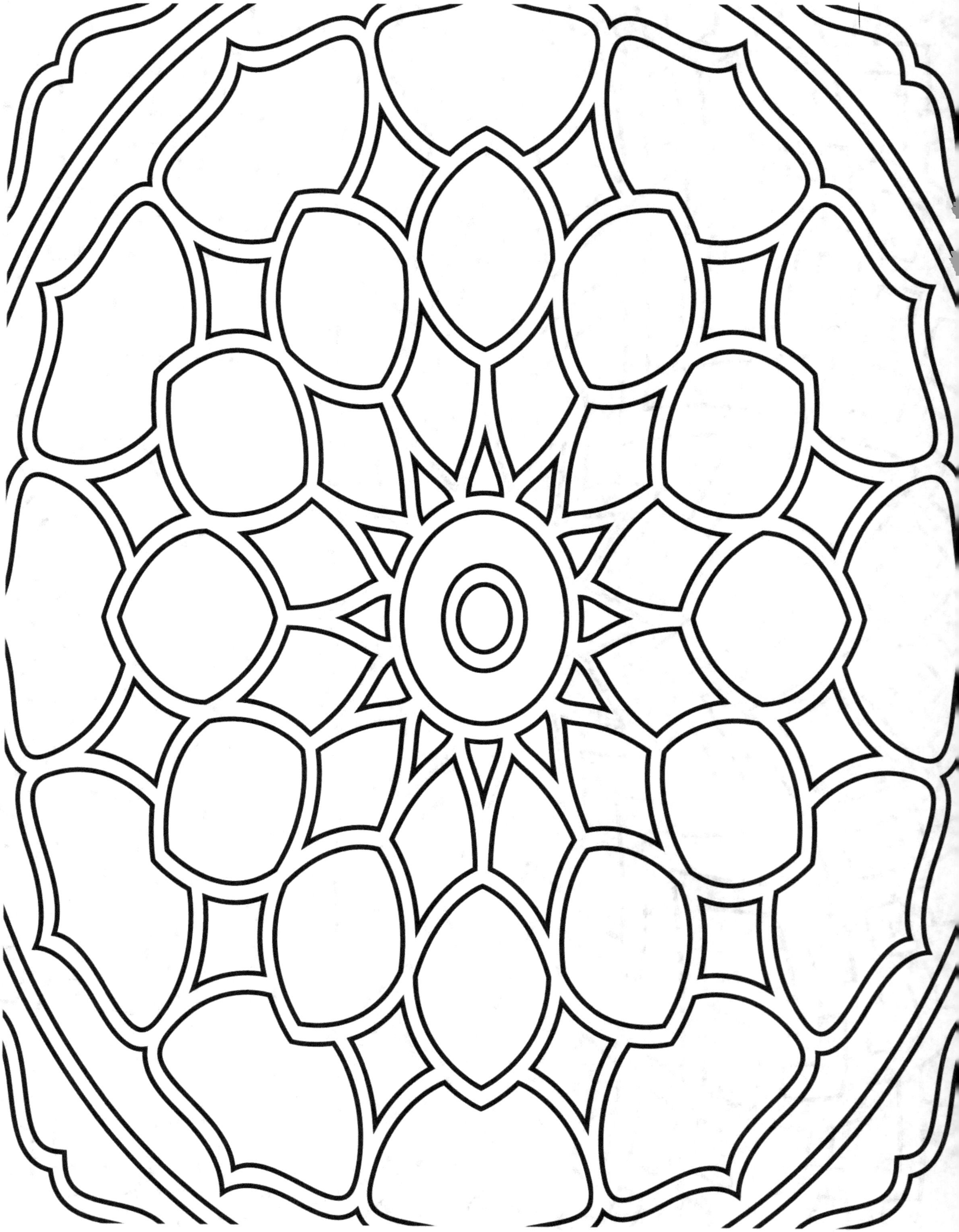

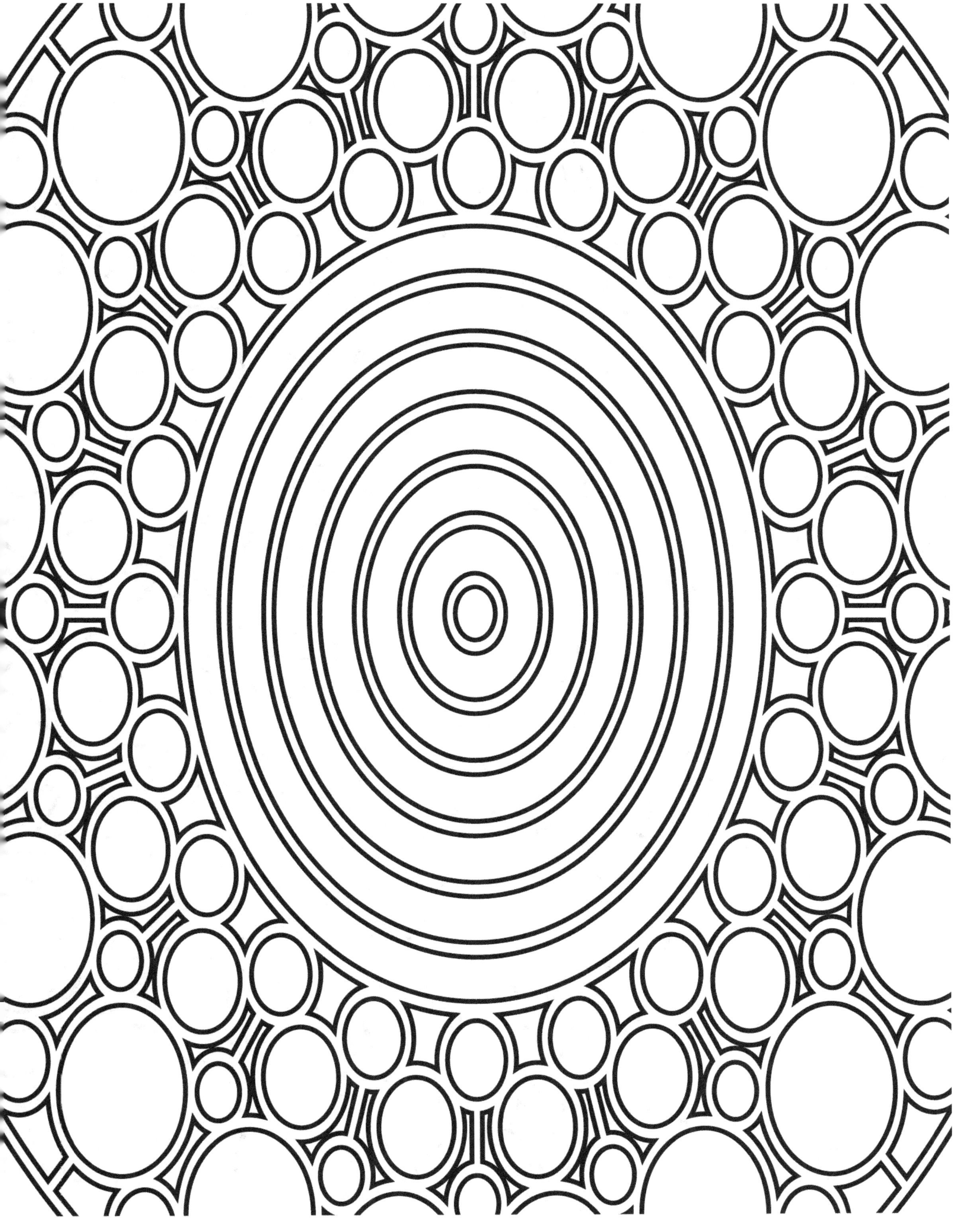

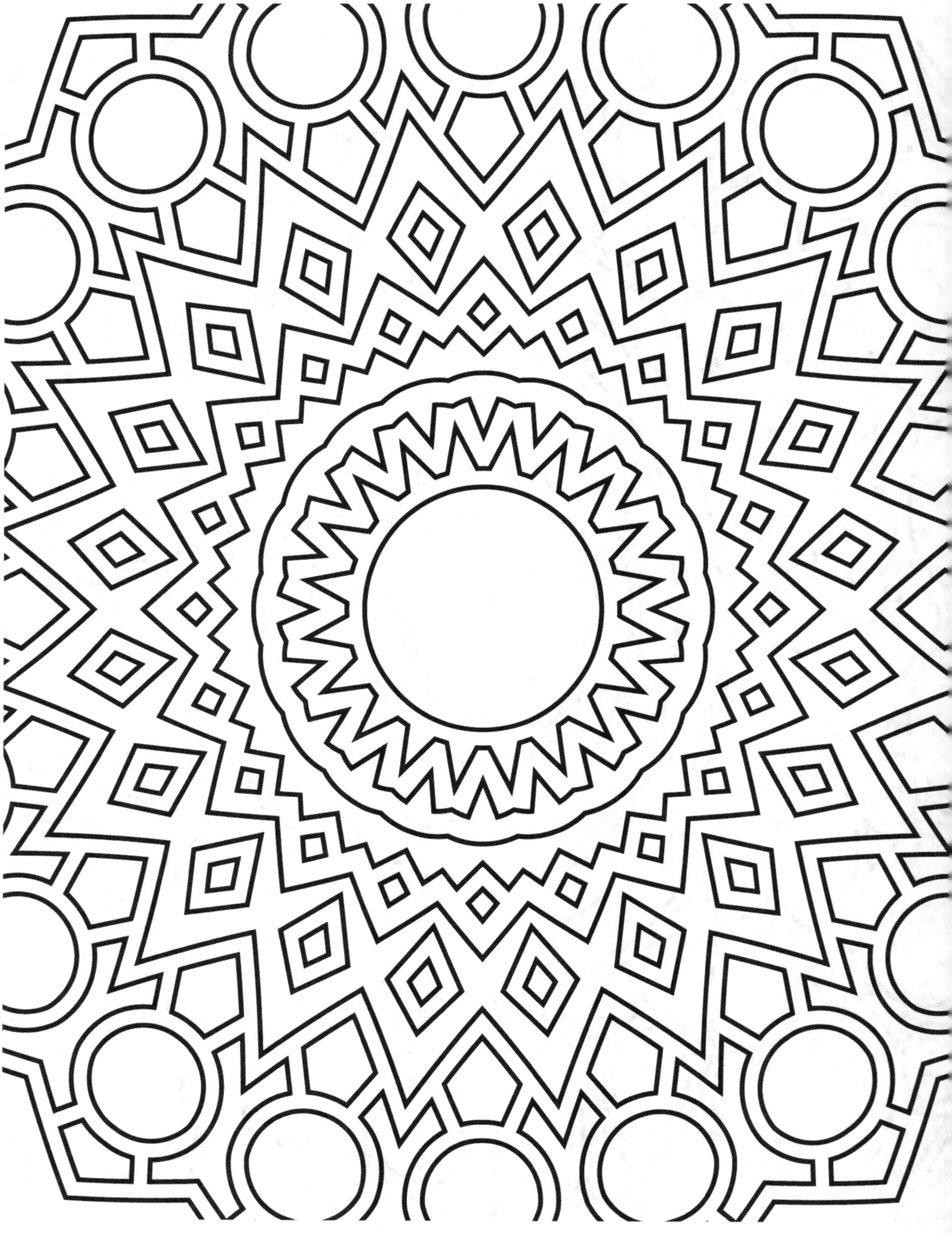

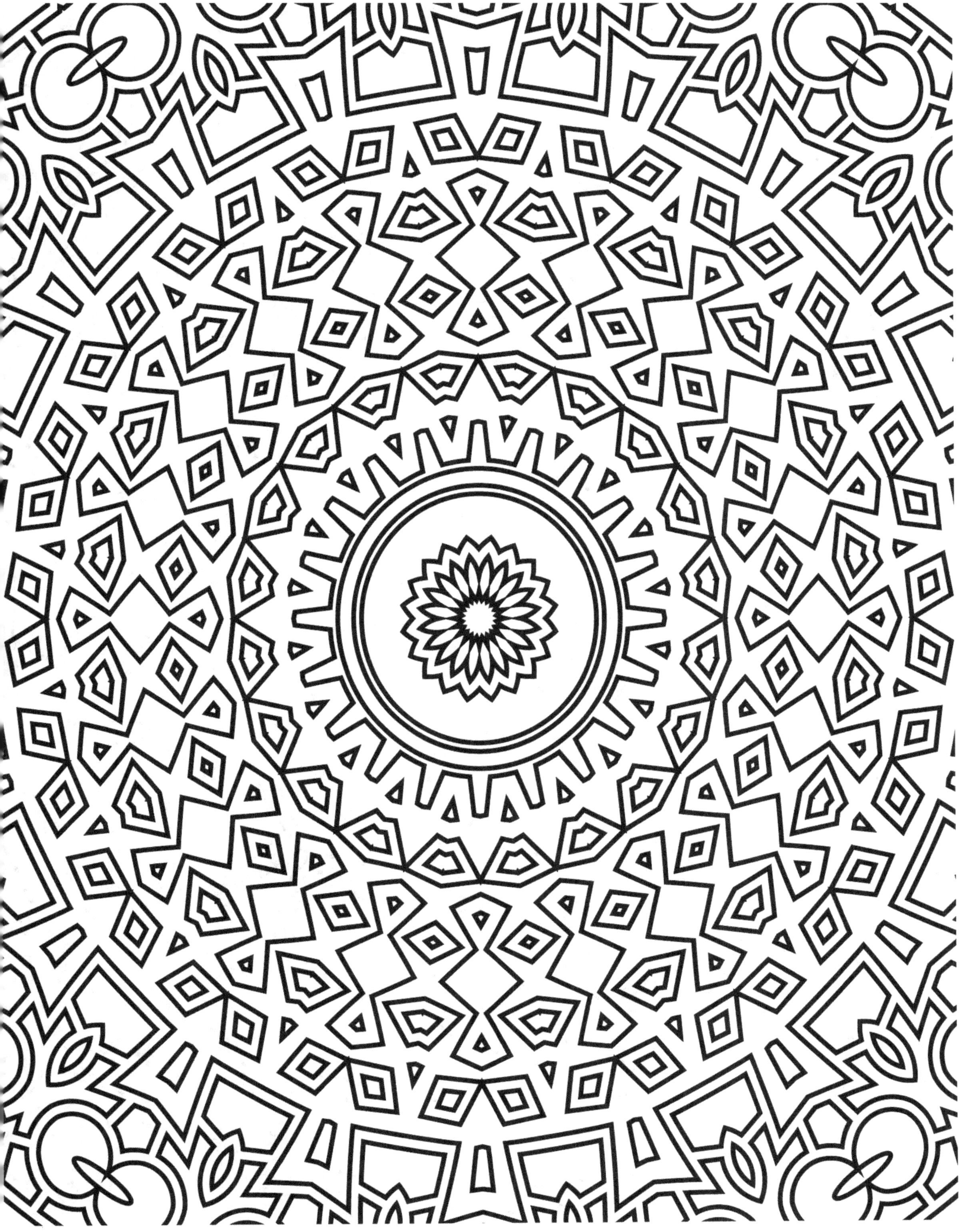

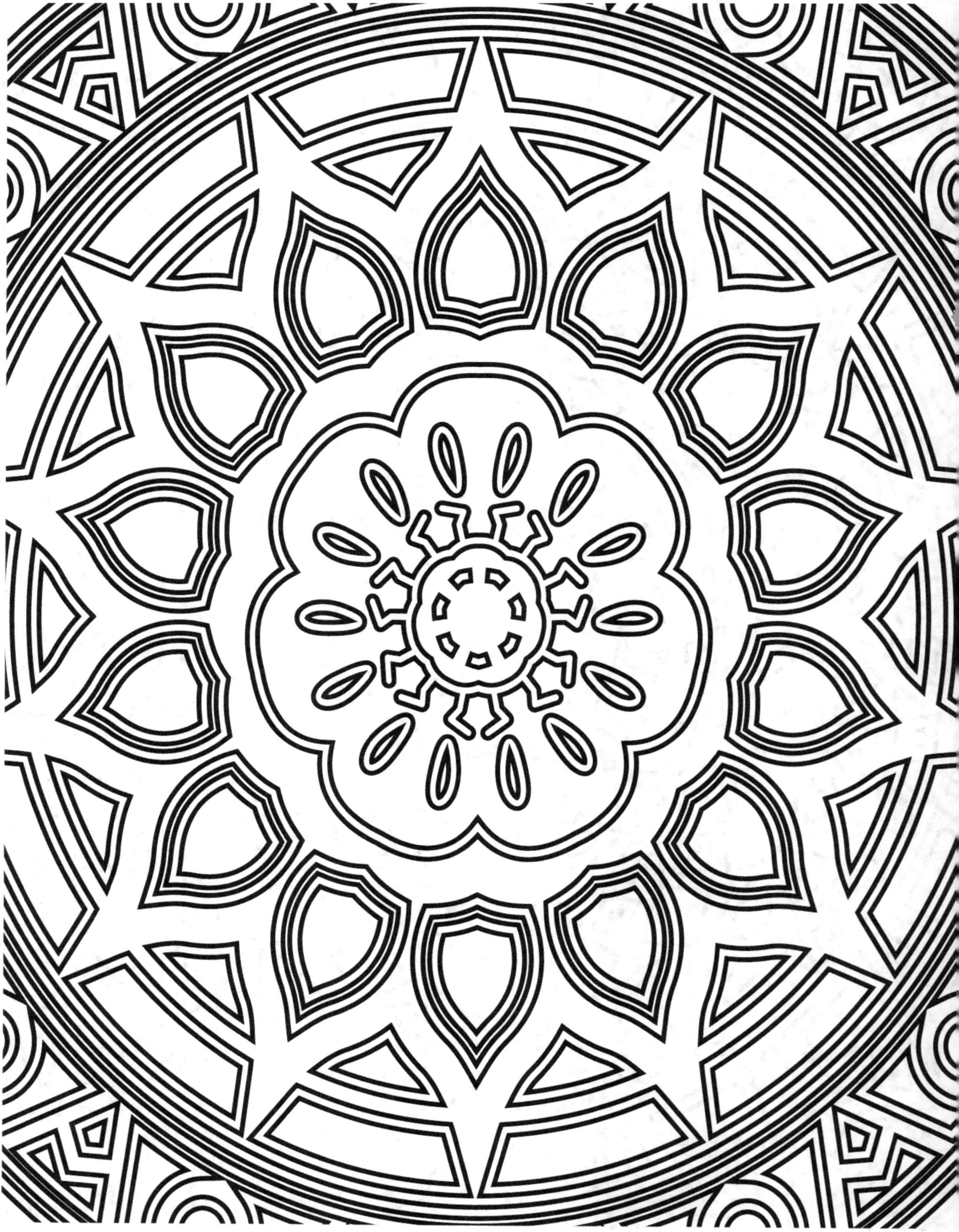

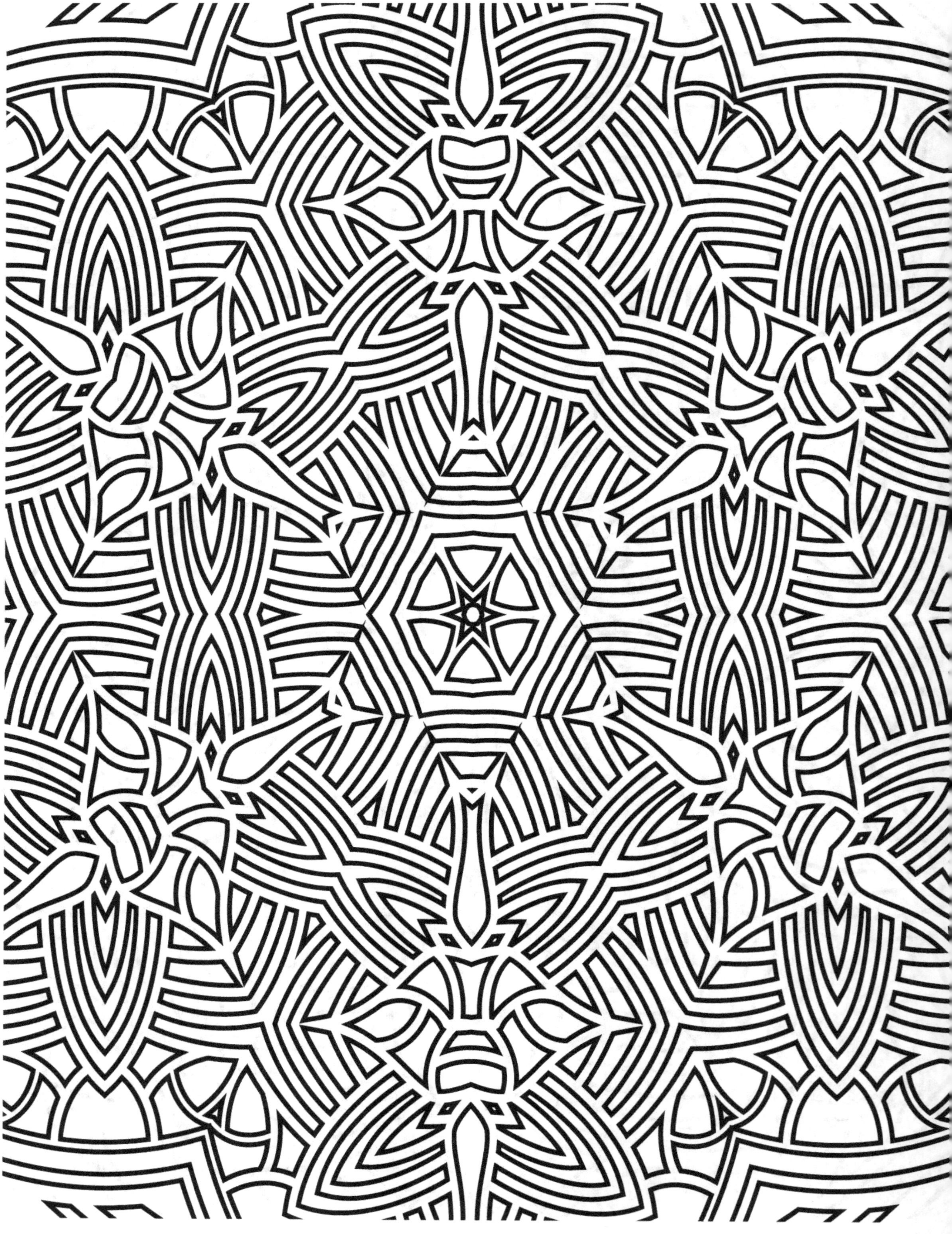

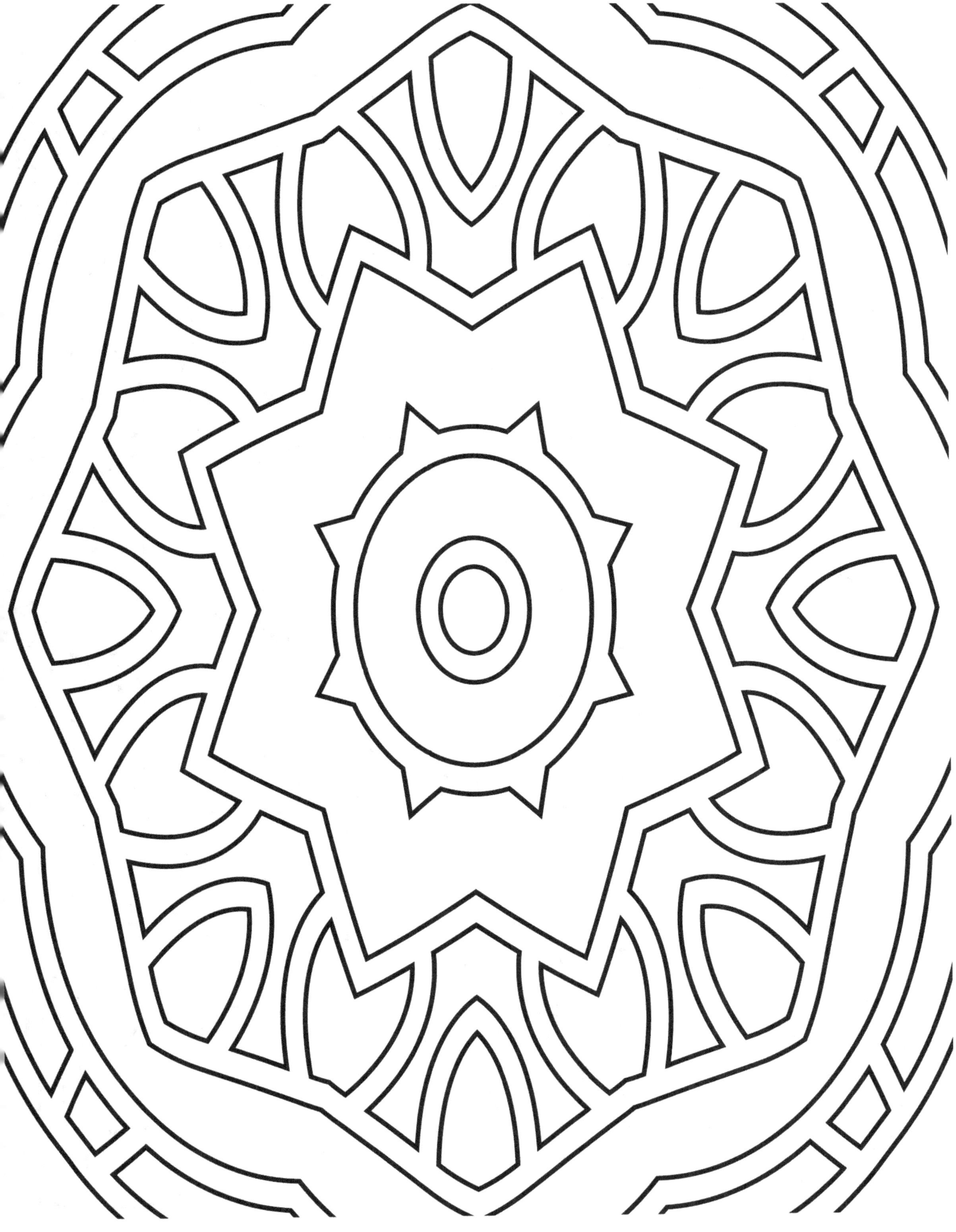

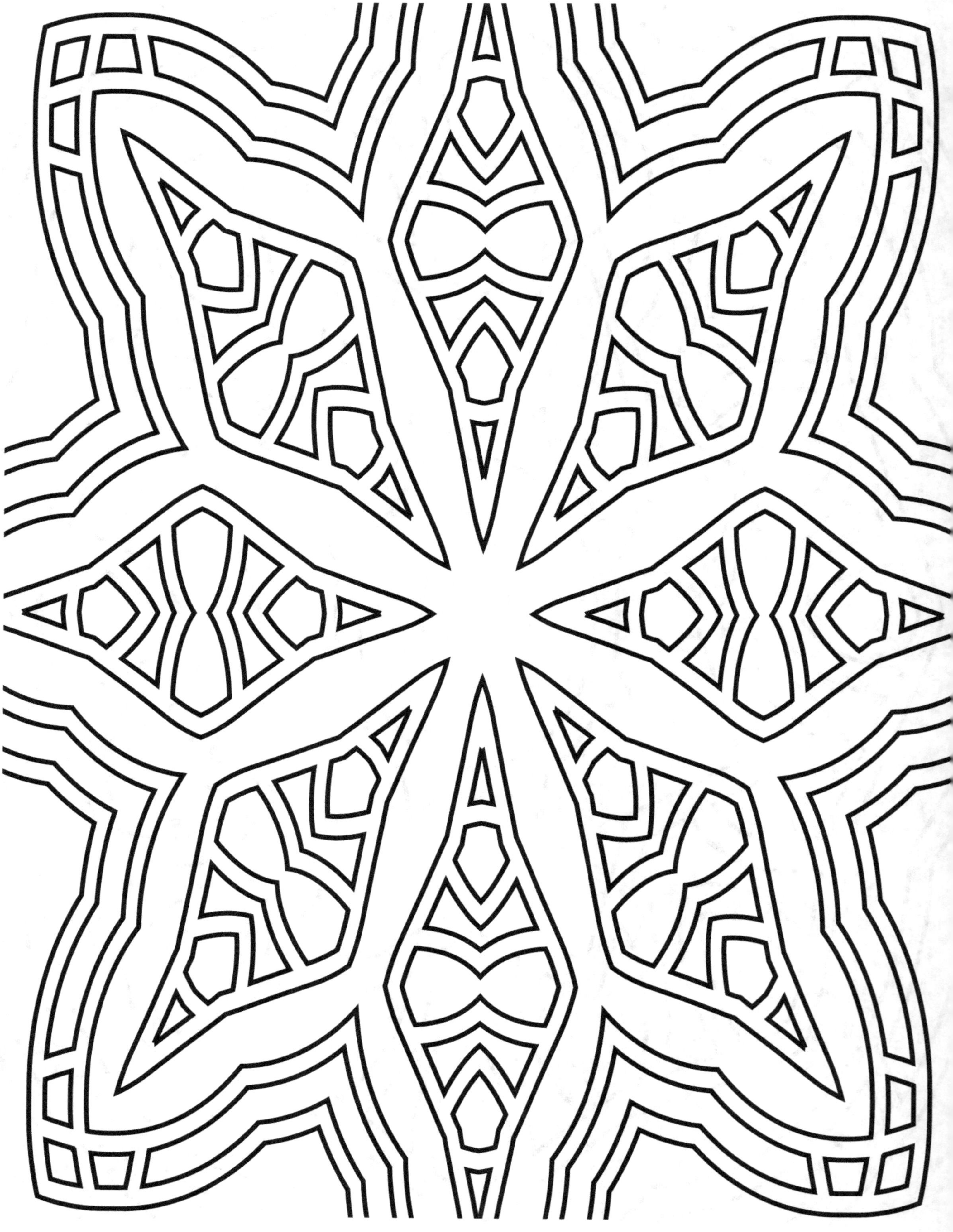

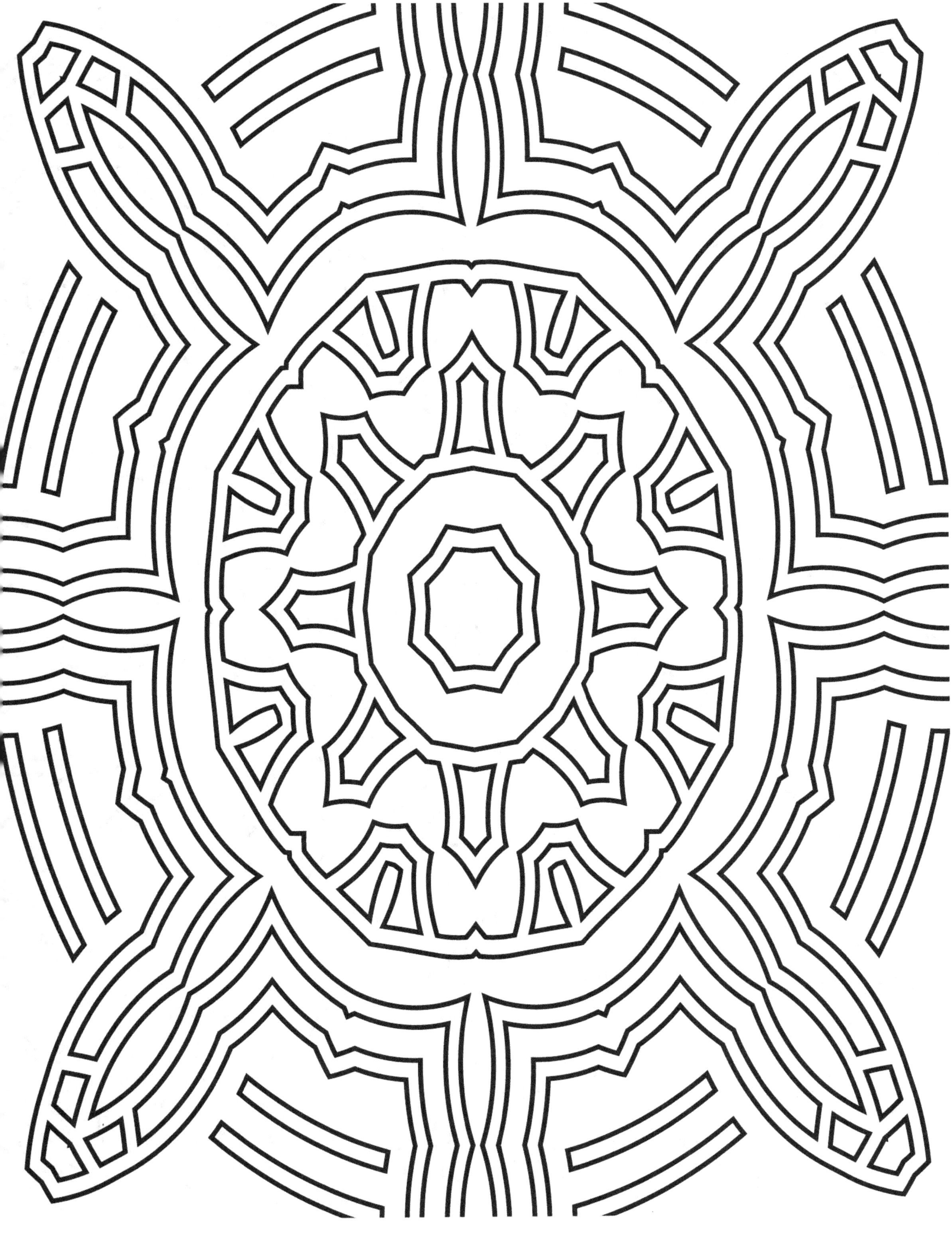

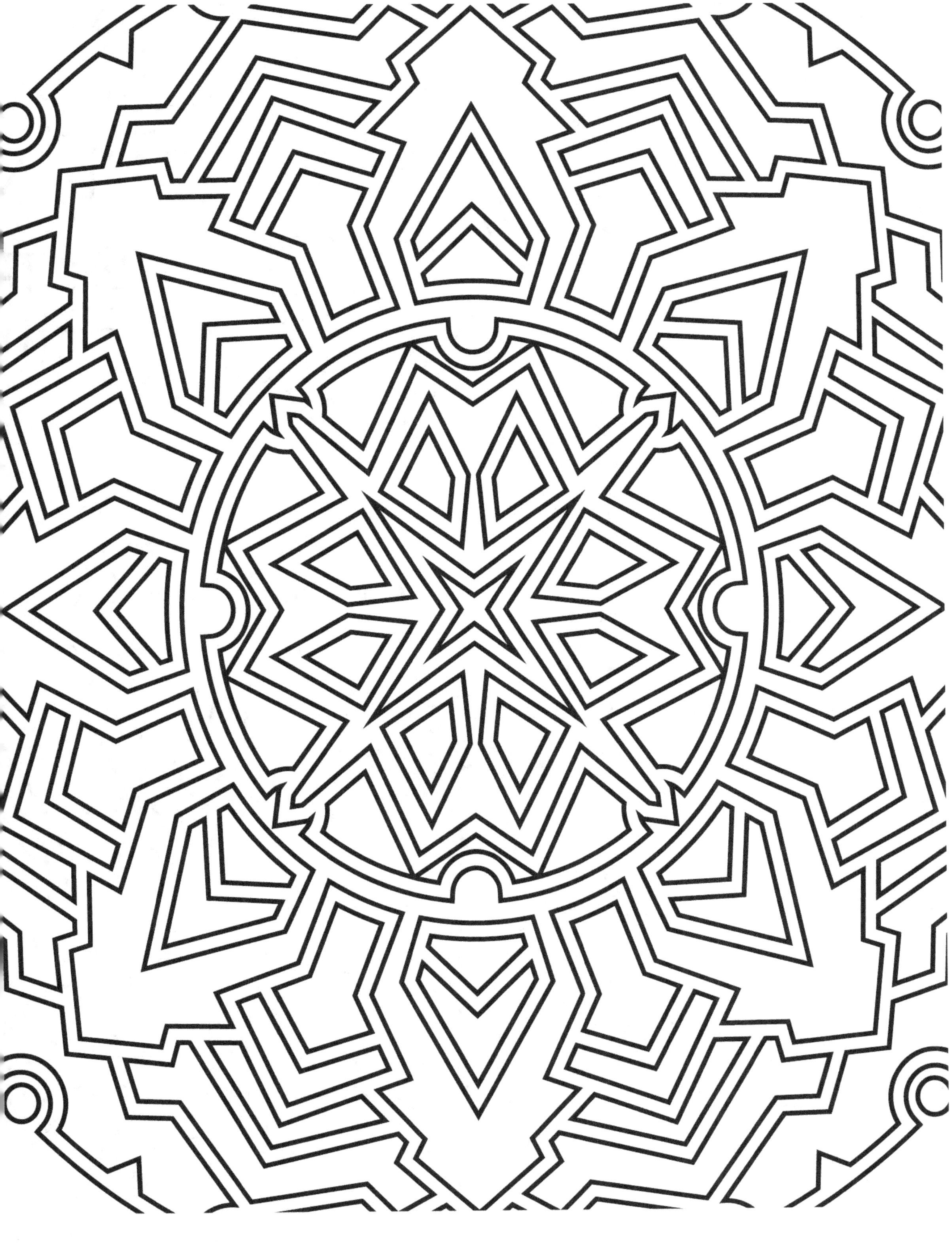

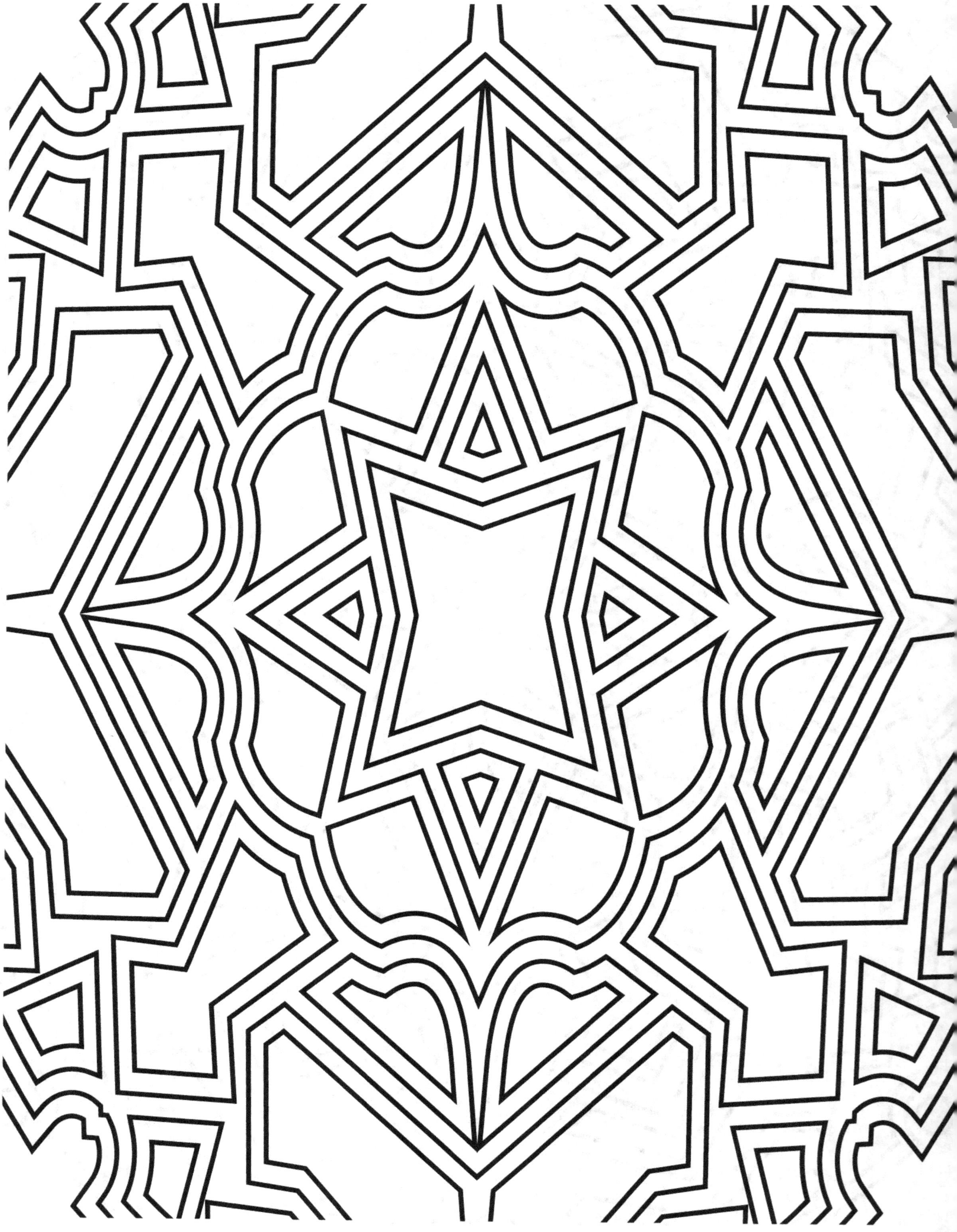

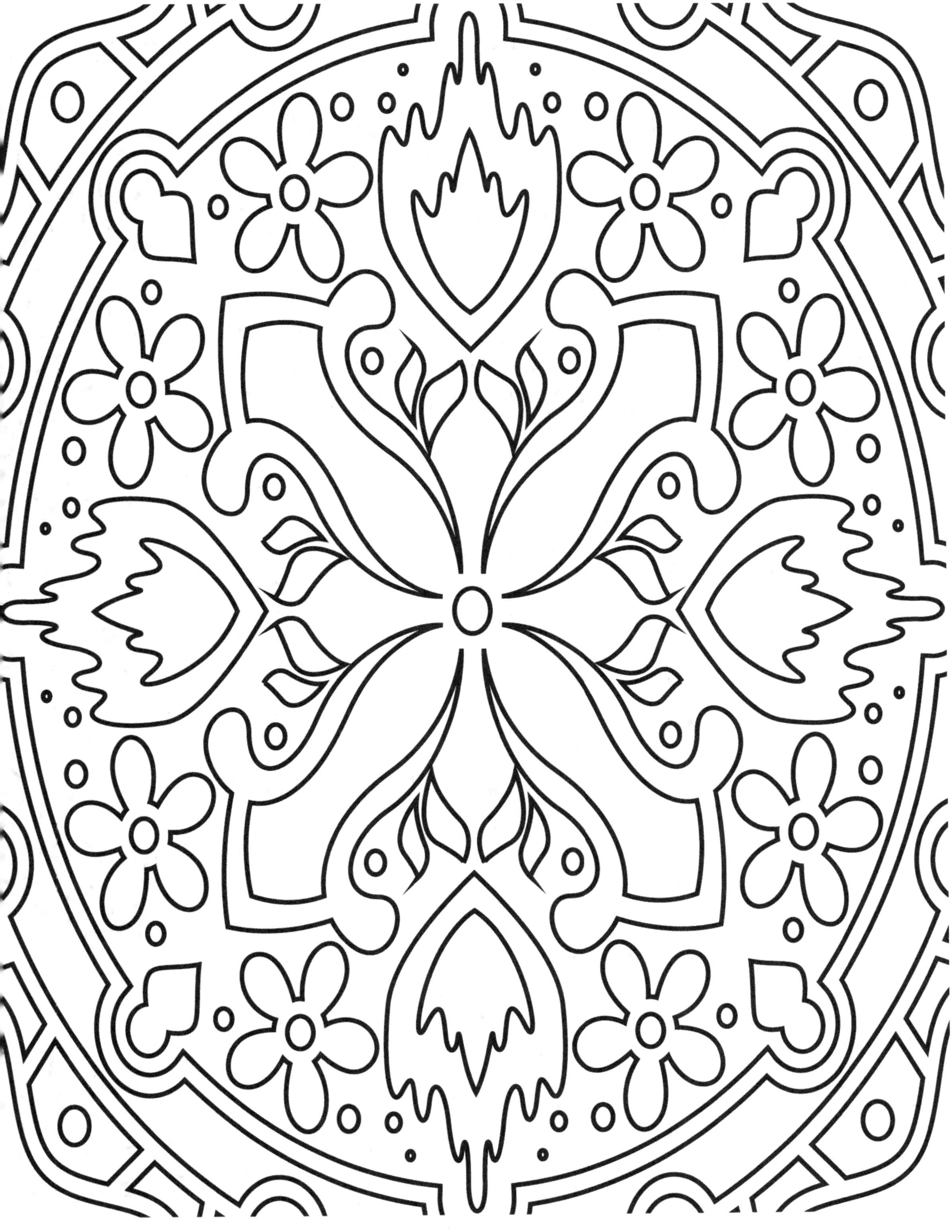

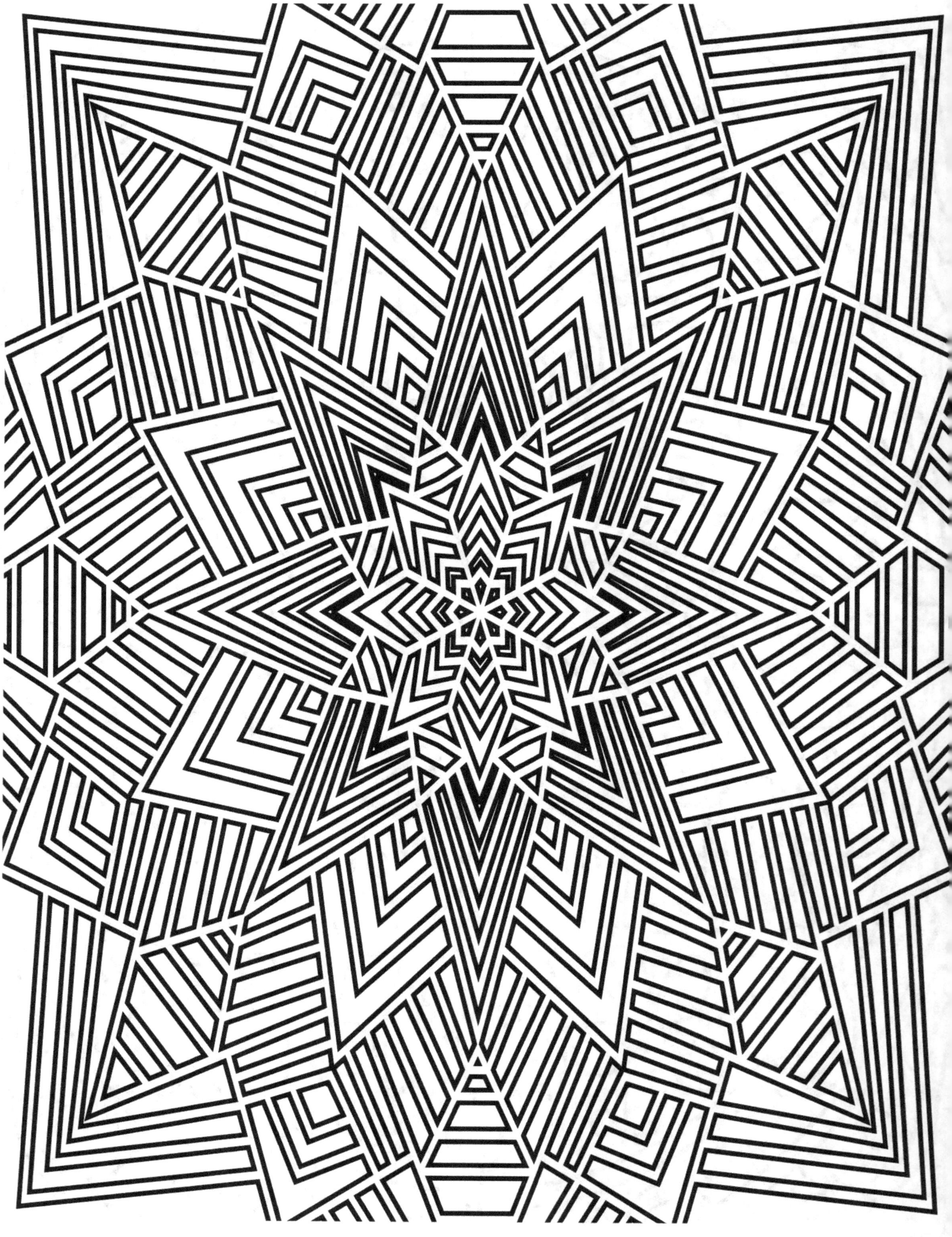

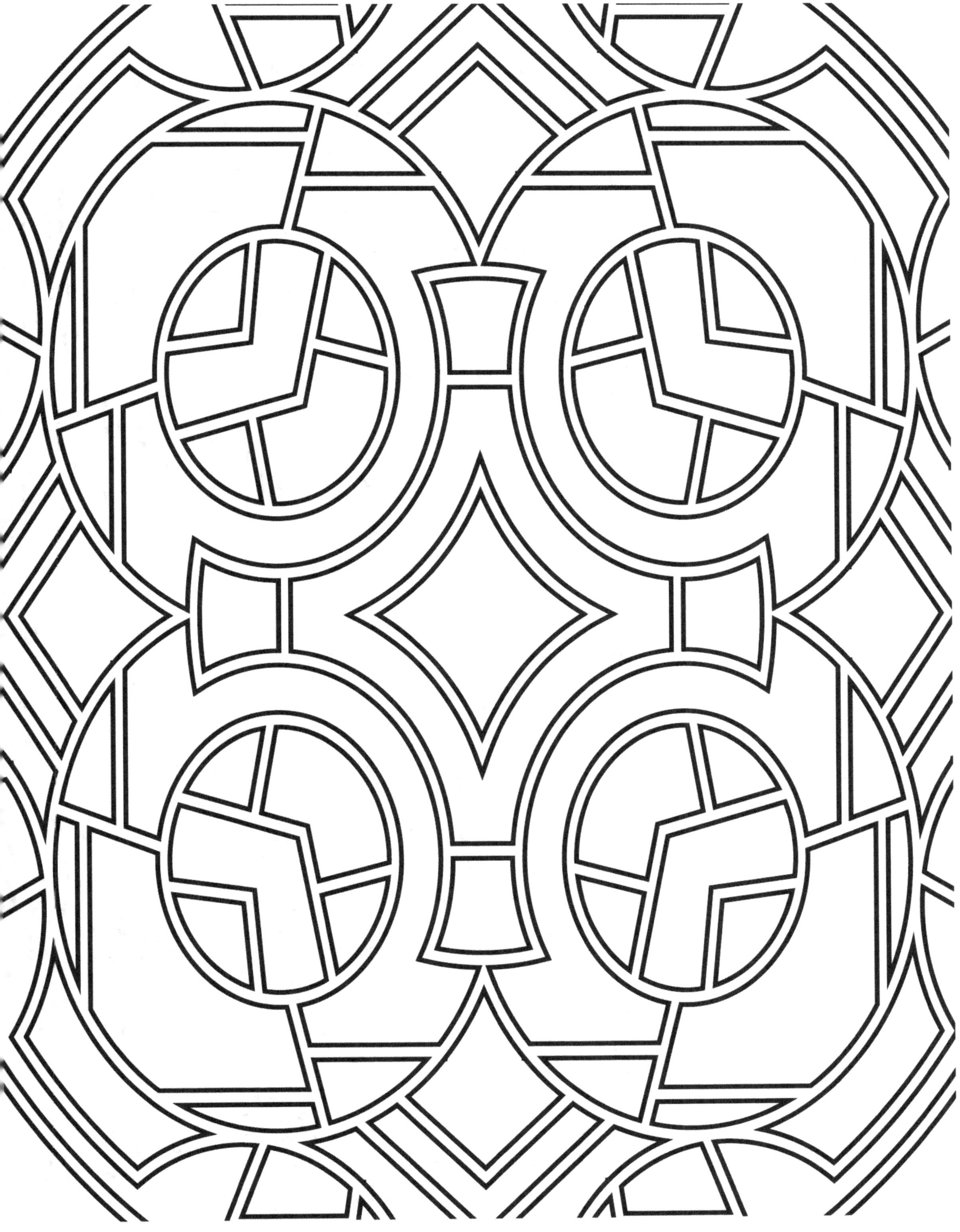

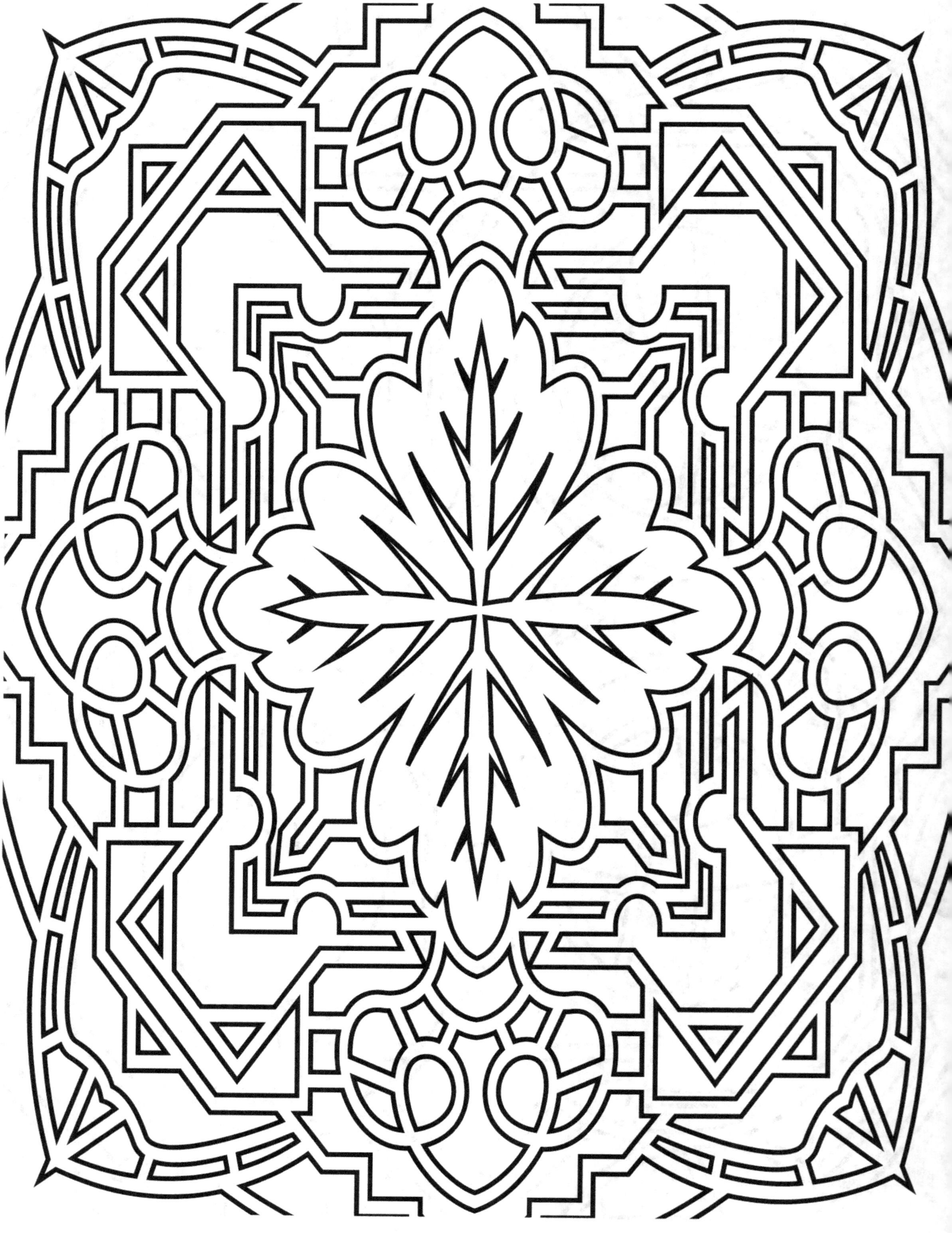

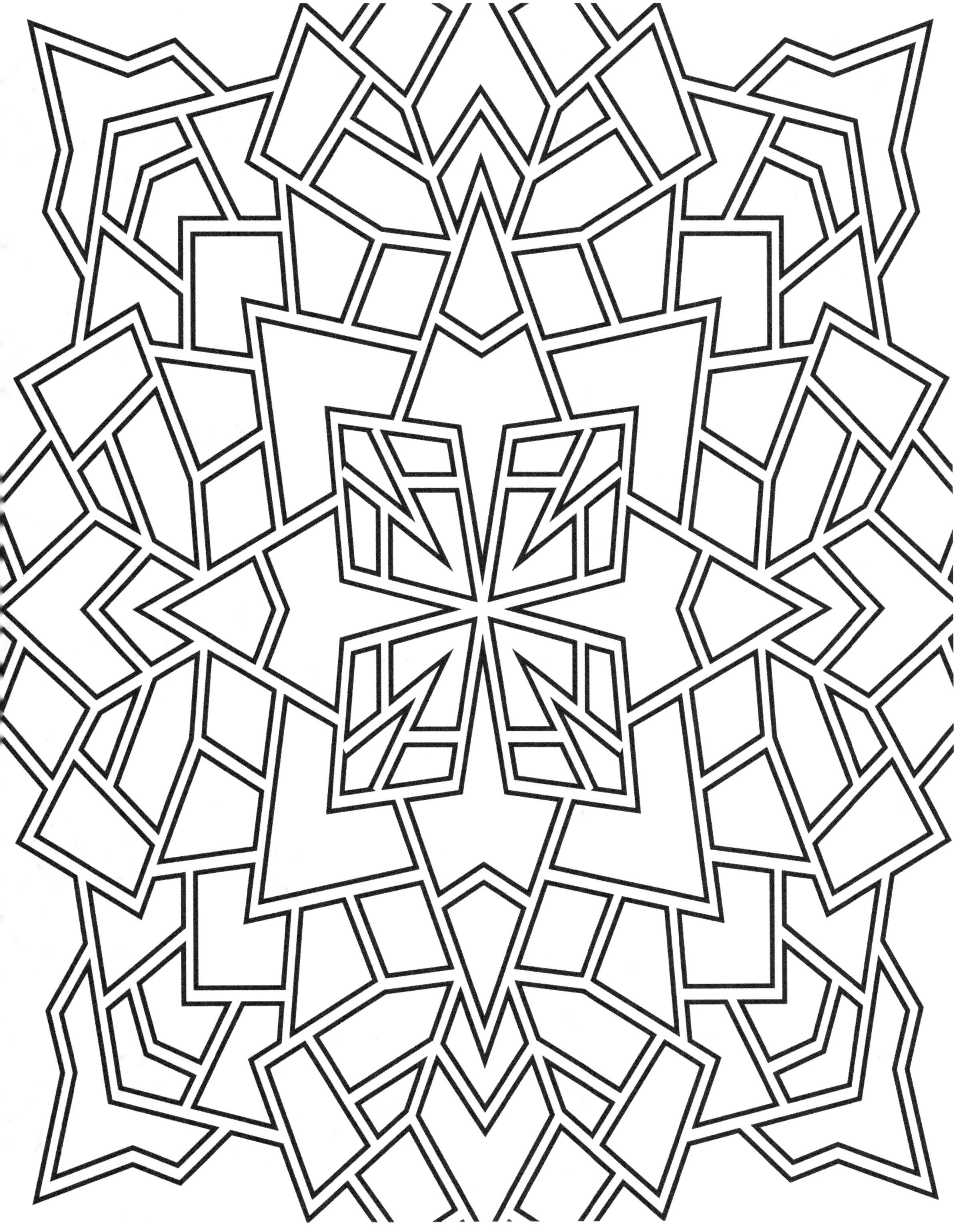

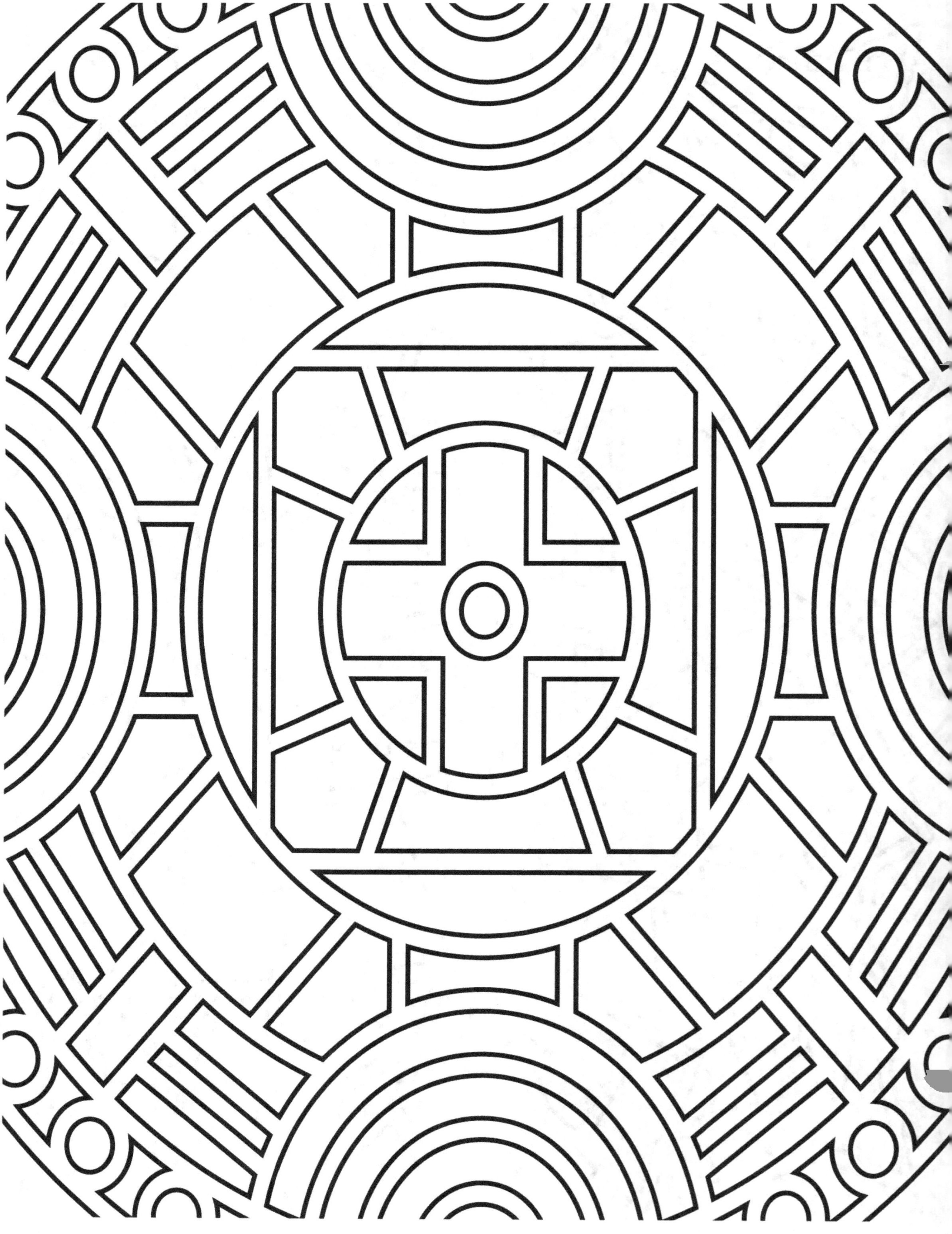

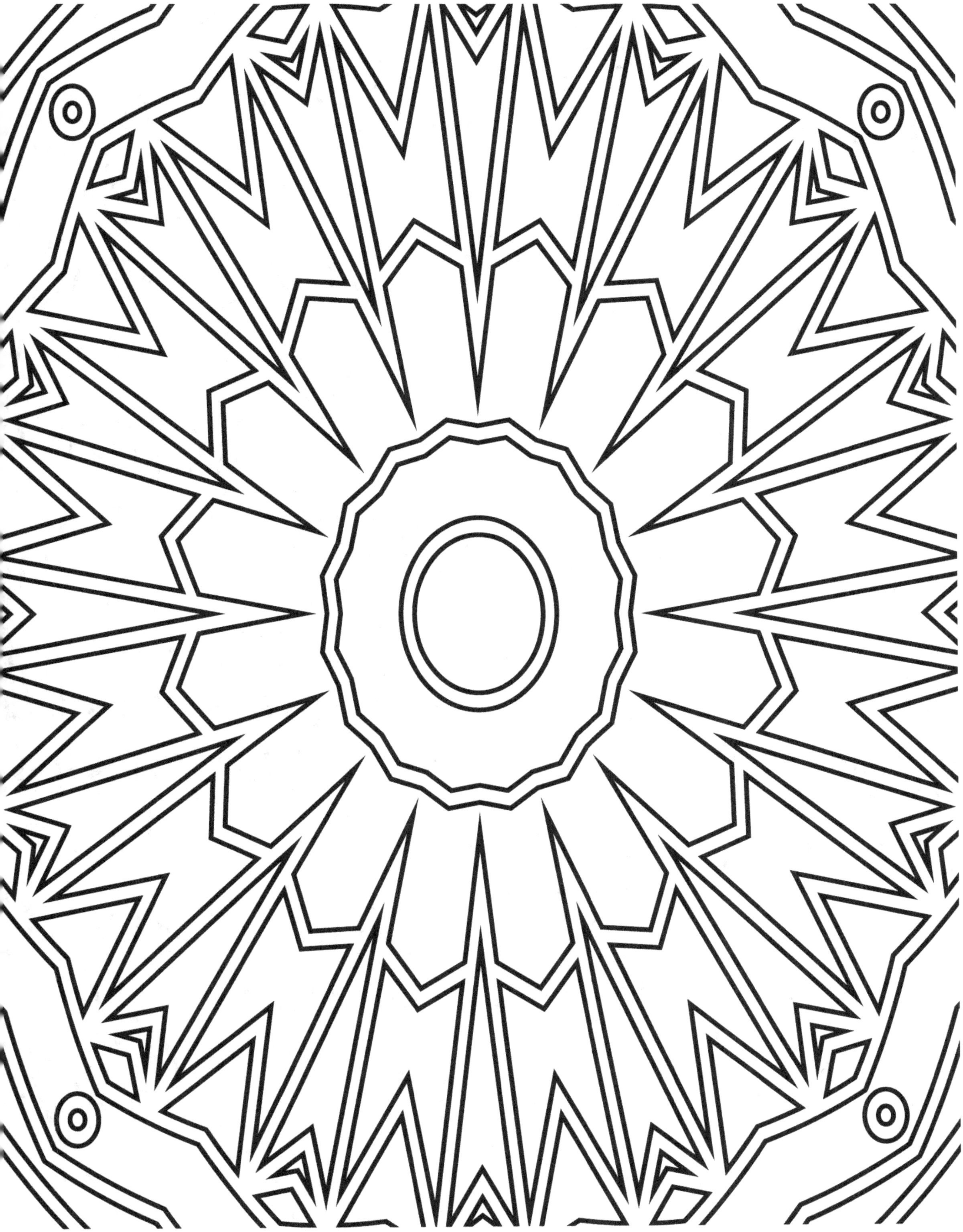

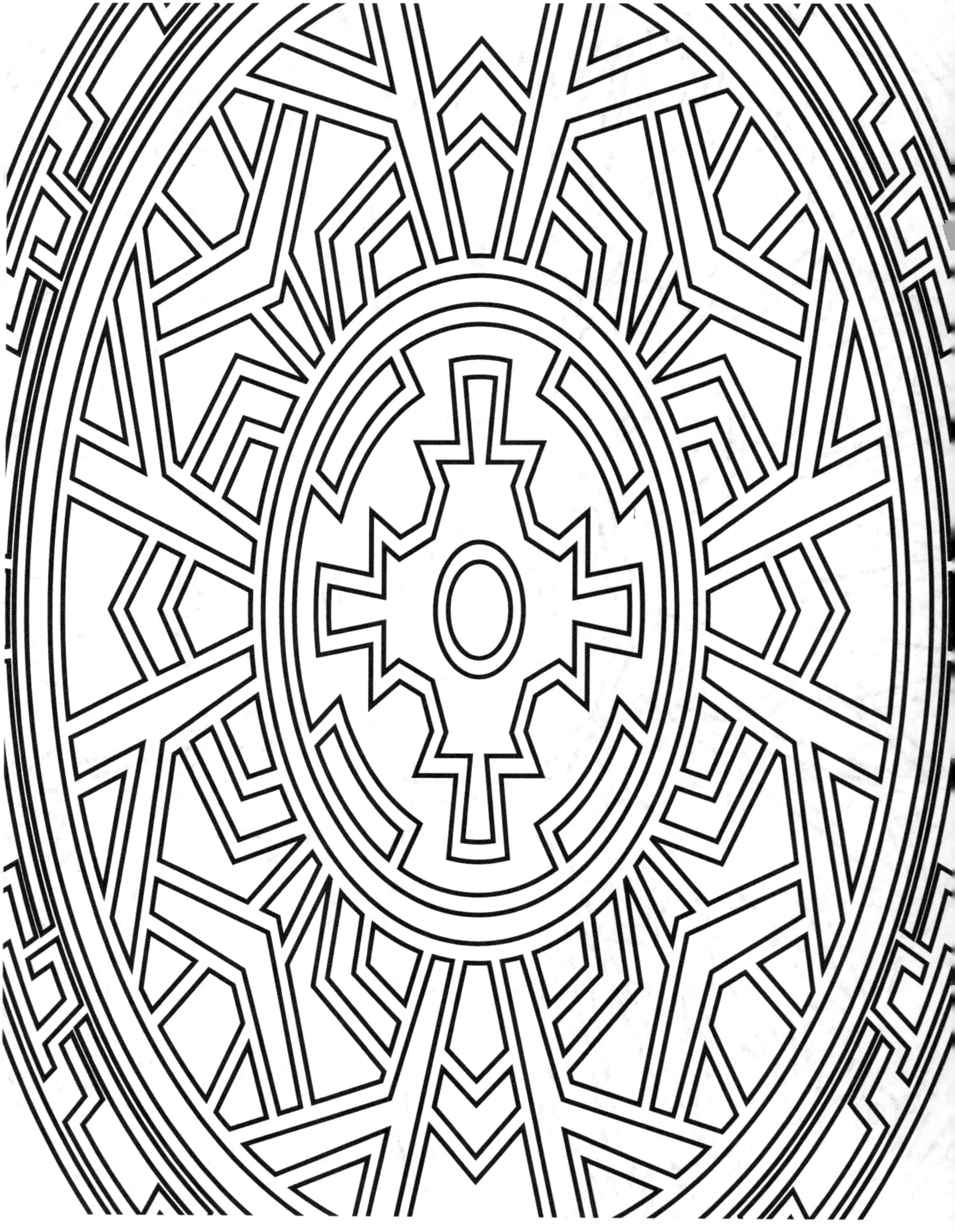

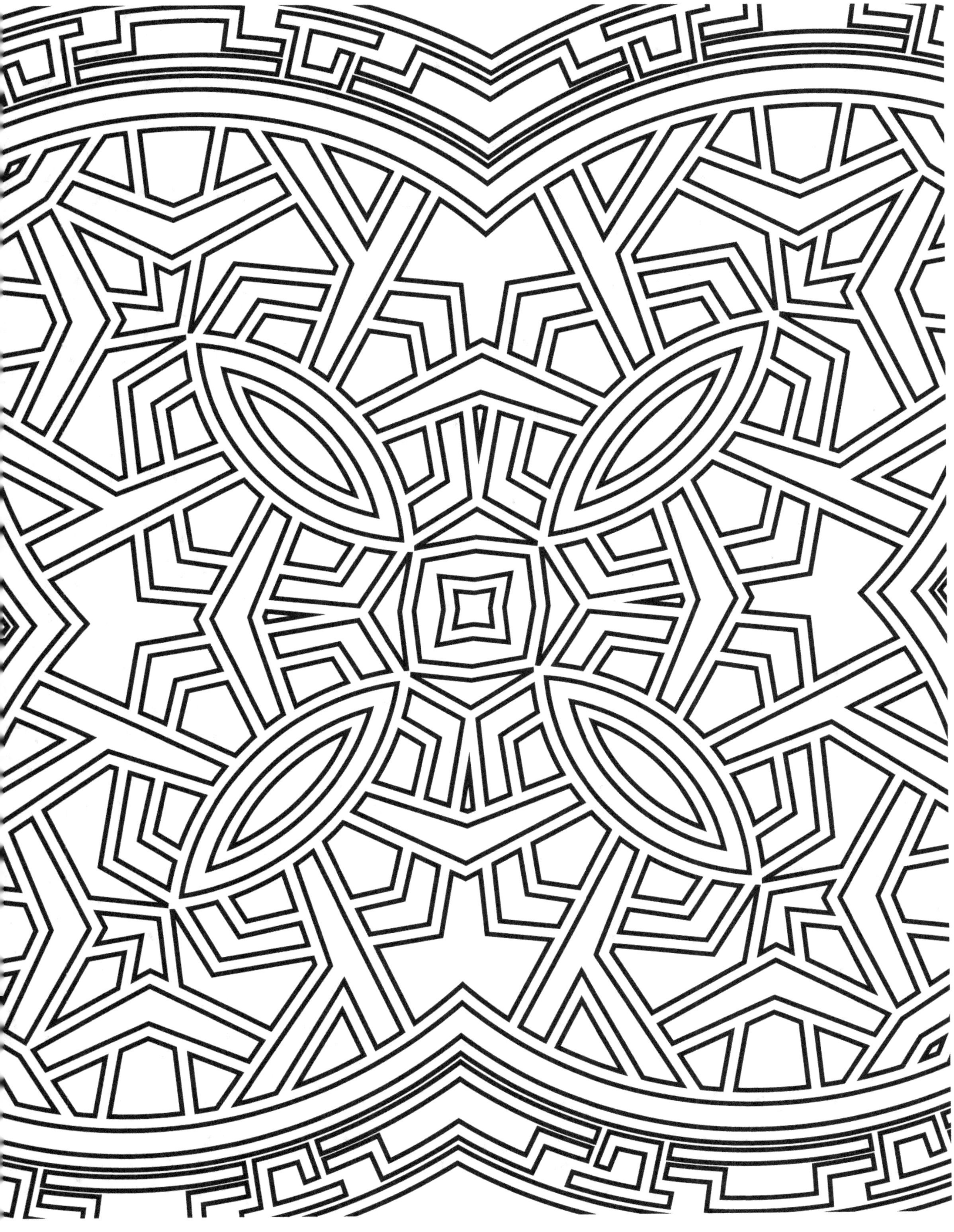

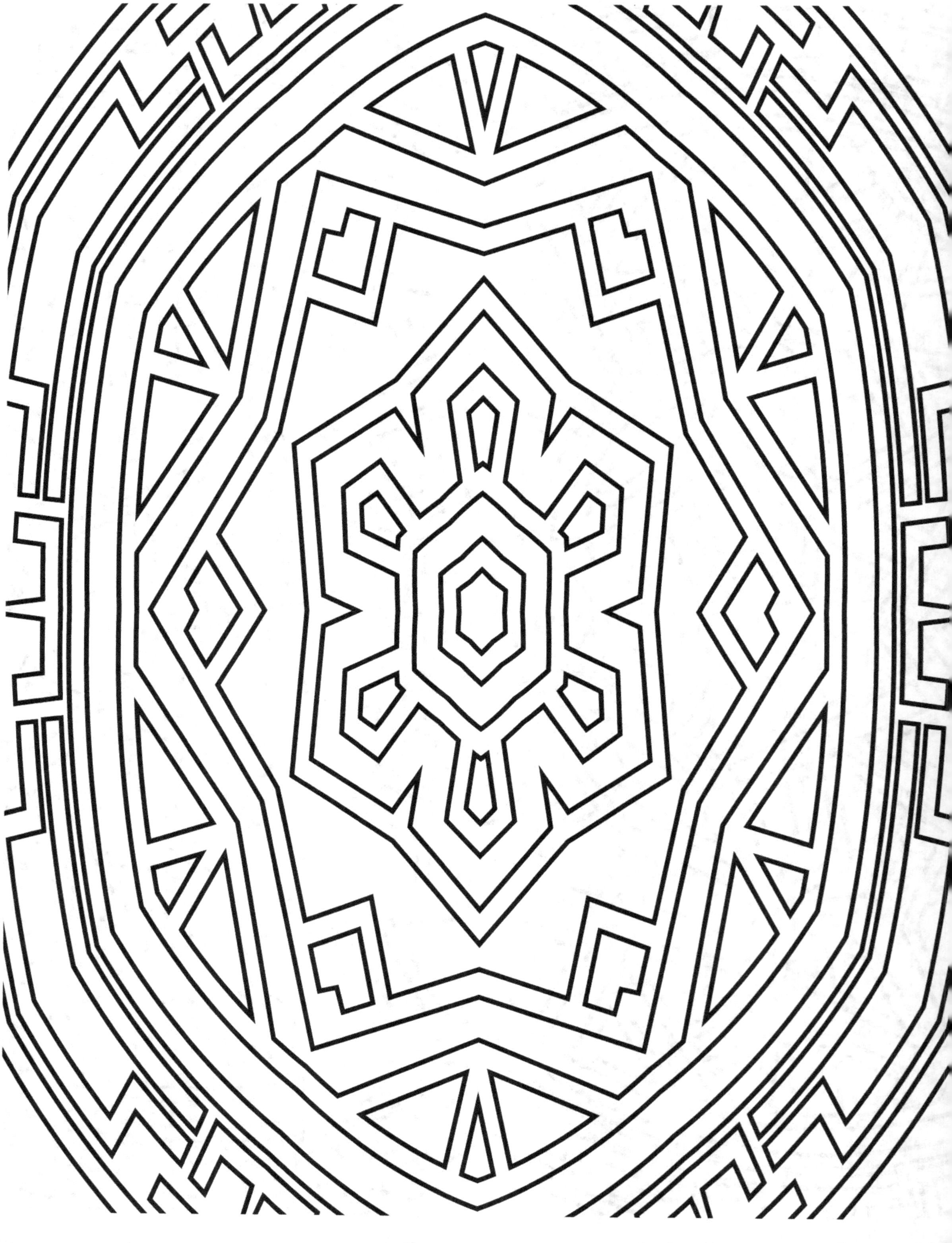

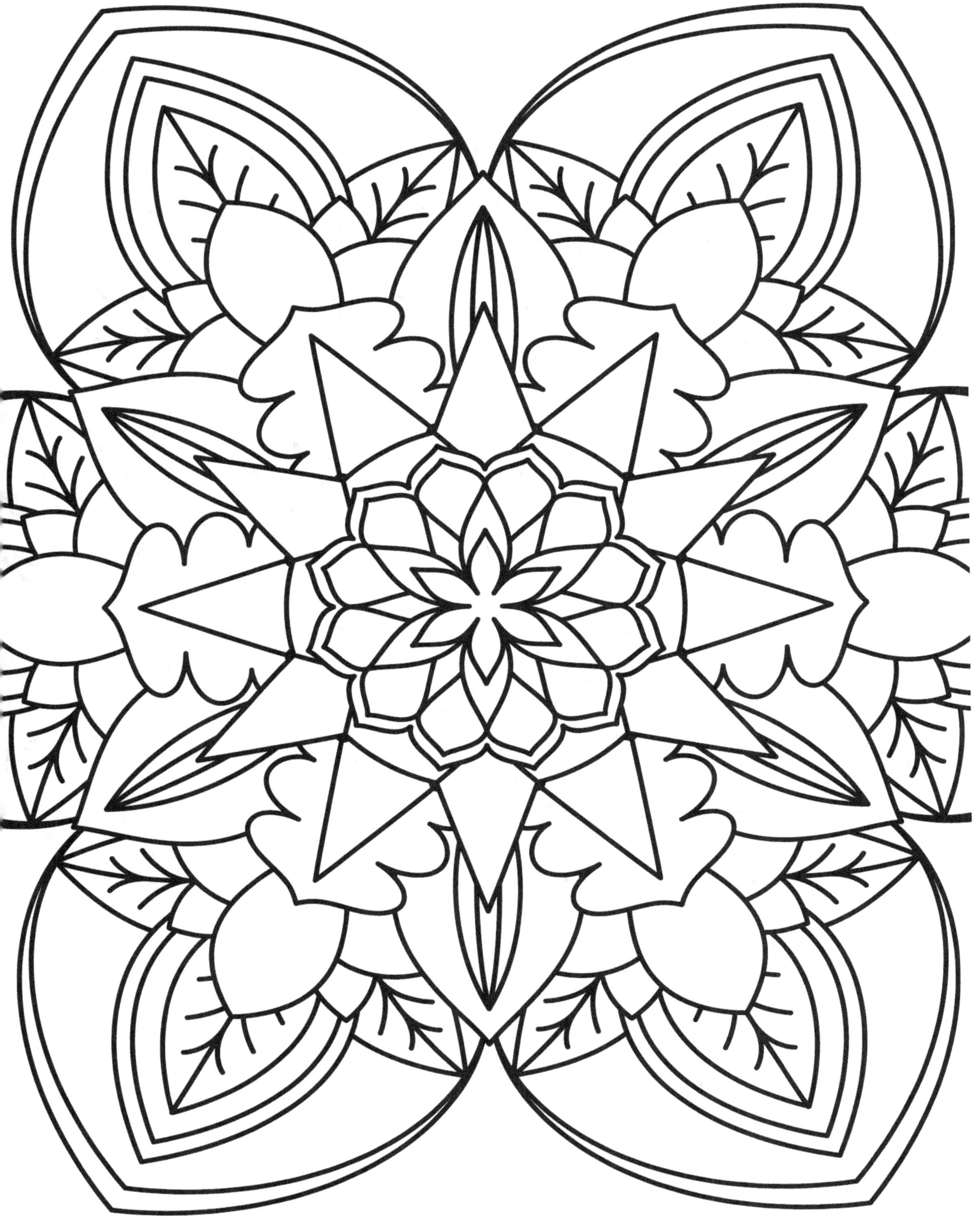

www.ingramcontent.com/pod-product-compliance
Lightning Source LLC
Chambersburg PA
CBHW080937220526
45465CB00008BA/3075
* 9 7 9 8 6 5 3 8 7 0 7 4 3 *